Contents

Confessions of an English Opium-Eater

NOTICE TO THE READER

The incidents recorded in the preliminary *Confessions* lie within a period of which the earlier extreme is now rather more – and the latter extreme less – than nineteen years ago. Consequently, in a popular way of computing dates, many of the incidents might be indifferently referred to a distance of eighteen or of nineteen years – and, as the notes and memoranda for this narrative were drawn up originally about last Christmas, it seemed most natural in all cases to prefer the former date. In the hurry of composing the narrative, though some months had then elapsed, this date was everywhere retained – and, in many cases, perhaps, it leads to no error, or to none of importance. But in one instance, viz. where the author speaks of his own birthday, this adoption of one uniform date has led to a positive inaccuracy of an entire year: for, during the very time of composition, the nineteenth year from the earlier term of the whole period revolved to its close. It is, therefore, judged proper to mention that the period of that narrative lies between the early part of July 1802 and the beginning or middle of March 1803.

– Oct. 1, 1821.

TO THE READER

I HERE PRESENT YOU, courteous reader, with the record of a remarkable period in my life. According to my application of it, I trust that it will prove not merely an interesting record, but, in a considerable degree, useful and instructive. In *that* hope it is that I have drawn it up, and *that* must be my apology for breaking through that delicate and honourable reserve which, for the most part, restrains us from the public exposure of our own errors and infirmities. Nothing, indeed, is more revolting to English feelings than the spectacle of a human being obtruding on our notice his moral ulcers or scars, and tearing away that "decent drapery"* which time, or indulgence to human frailty, may have drawn over them. Accordingly, the greater part of *our* confessions (that is, spontaneous and extrajudicial confessions) proceed from demi-reps,* adventurers or swindlers, and for any such acts of gratuitous self-humiliation from those who can be supposed in sympathy with the decent and self-respecting part of society, we must look to French literature, or to that part of the German which is tainted with the spurious and defective sensibility of the French.* All this I feel so forcibly, and so nervously am I alive to reproach of this tendency, that I have for many months hesitated about the propriety of allowing this or any part of my narrative to come before the public eye until after my death (when, for many reasons, the whole will be published), and it is not without an anxious review of the reasons for and against this step that I have, at last, concluded on taking it.

Guilt and misery shrink, by a natural instinct, from public notice: they court privacy and solitude, and even in their choice of a grave will sometimes sequester themselves from the general population of the churchyard, as if declining to claim fellowship with the great family of man, and wishing (in the affecting language of Mr Wordsworth)

> ...Humbly to express
> A penitential loneliness.*

It is well, upon the whole, and for the interest of us all, that it should be so; nor would I willingly, in my own person, manifest a disregard of such salutary feelings; nor in act or word do anything to weaken them. But, on the one hand, as my self-accusation does not amount to a confession of guilt, so, on the other, it is possible that, if it *did*, the benefit resulting to others, from the record of an experience purchased at so heavy a price, might compensate, by a vast overbalance, for any violence done to the feelings I have noticed and justify a breach of the general rule. Infirmity and misery do not, of necessity, imply guilt. They approach, or recede from, the shades of that dark alliance in proportion to the probable motives and prospects of the offender, and the palliations, known or secret, of the offence, in proportion as the temptations to it were potent from the first, and the resistance to it, in act or in effort, was earnest to the last. For my own part, without breach of truth or modesty, I may affirm that my life has been, on the whole, the life of a philosopher: from my birth I was made an intellectual creature, and intellectual in the highest sense my pursuits and pleasures have been, even from my schoolboy days. If opium-eating be a sensual pleasure, and if I am bound to confess that I have indulged in it to an excess not yet *recorded** of any other man, it is no less true that I have struggled against this fascinating enthralment with a religious zeal, and have, at length, accomplished what I never yet heard attributed to any other man – have untwisted, almost to its final links, the accursed chain which fettered me. Such a self-conquest may reasonably be set off in counterbalance to any kind or degree of self-indulgence. Not to insist that, in my case, the self-conquest was unquestionable, the self-indulgence open to doubts of casuistry, according as that name shall be extended to acts aiming at the bare relief of pain, or shall be restricted to such as aim at the excitement of positive pleasure.

Guilt, therefore, I do not acknowledge, and if I did, it is possible that I might still resolve on the present act of confession, in consideration of the service which I may thereby render to the whole class of opium-eaters. But who are they? Reader, I am sorry to say a very numerous class indeed. Of this I became convinced some years ago, by computing, at that time, the number of those in one small class of English society (the class of men distinguished for talents, or of eminent station) who were known to me, directly or indirectly, as opium-eaters; such, for instance, as the eloquent and benevolent ——, the late Dean of ——, Lord ——, Mr ——, the philosopher, a late under-secretary of state (who described to me the sensation which first drove him to the use of opium in the very same words as the Dean of ——, viz. "that he felt as though rats were gnawing and abrading the coats of his stomach"), Mr ——* and many others, hardly less known, whom it would be tedious to mention. Now, if one class, comparatively so limited, could furnish so many scores of cases (and *that* within the knowledge of one single enquirer), it was a natural inference that the entire population of England would furnish a proportionable number. The soundness of this inference, however, I doubted until some facts became known to me which satisfied me that it was not incorrect. I will mention two: 1. Three respectable London druggists, in widely remote quarters of London, from whom I happened lately to be purchasing small quantities of opium, assured me that the number of *amateur* opium-eaters (as I may term them) was, at this time, immense, and that the difficulty of distinguishing these persons, to whom habit had rendered opium necessary, from such as were purchasing it with a view to suicide,* occasioned them daily trouble and disputes. This evidence respected London only. But, 2. (which will possibly surprise the reader more) Some years ago, on passing through Manchester, I was informed by several cotton manufacturers that their workpeople were rapidly getting into the practice of opium-eating – so much so that on a Saturday afternoon the counters of the druggists were strewed with pills of one, two or three grains, in preparation for the known demand of the evening. The immediate occasion of this practice was the lowness of wages, which, at that time, would not allow them to indulge in ale or spirits; and, wages rising, it may be thought that this practice would cease, but, as I do not readily believe that any man, having once tasted the divine luxuries of opium, will afterwards descend to the gross and mortal enjoyments of alcohol, I take it for granted

> That those eat now who never ate before,
> And those who always ate now eat the more.*

Indeed the fascinating powers of opium are admitted even by medical writers, who are its greatest enemies. Thus, for instance, Awsiter, apothecary to Greenwich Hospital, in his 'Essay on the Effects of Opium' (published in the year 1763), when attempting to explain why Mead* had not been sufficiently explicit on the properties, counteragents, etc., of this drug, expresses himself in the following mysterious terms (φωνᾶντα συνετοῖσι):* "Perhaps he thought the subject of too delicate a nature to be made common; and as many people might then indiscriminately use it, it would take from that necessary fear and caution which should prevent their experiencing the extensive power of this drug: *for there are many properties in it, if universally known, that would habituate the use and make it more in request with us than the Turks themselves*. The result of which knowledge," he adds, "must prove a general misfortune." In the necessity of this conclusion I do not altogether concur, but upon that point I shall have occasion to speak at the close of my confessions, where I shall present the reader with the *moral* of my narrative.

PART I: PRELIMINARY CONFESSIONS

THESE PRELIMINARY CONFESSIONS, or introductory narrative of the youthful adventures which laid the foundation of the writer's habit of opium-eating in after-life, it has been judged proper to premise for three several reasons:

1. As forestalling that question, and giving it a satisfactory answer, which else would painfully obtrude itself in the course of the 'Opium Confessions': "How came any reasonable being to subject himself to such a yoke of misery, voluntarily to incur a captivity so servile and knowingly to fetter himself with such a sevenfold chain?" A question which, if not somewhere plausibly resolved, could hardly

fail, by the indignation which it would be apt to raise as against an act of wanton folly, to interfere with that degree of sympathy which is necessary in any case to an author's purposes.

2. As furnishing a key to some parts of that tremendous scenery which afterwards peopled the dreams of the Opium-Eater.

3. As creating some previous interest of a personal sort in the confessing subject apart from the matter of the confessions, which cannot fail to render the confessions themselves more interesting. If a man "whose talk is of oxen"* should become an opium-eater, the probability is that (if he is not too dull to dream at all) he will dream about oxen; whereas, in the case before him, the reader will find that the Opium-Eater boasteth himself to be a philosopher, and accordingly that the phantasmagoria of *his* dreams (waking or sleeping, daydreams or night dreams) is suitable to one who in that character

*Humani nihil a se alienum putat.**

For amongst the conditions which he deems indispensable to the sustaining of any claim to the title of philosopher is not merely the possession of a superb intellect in its *analytic* functions (in which part of the pretension, however, England can for some generations show but few claimants – at least, he is not aware of any known candidate for this honour who can be styled emphatically *a subtle thinker*, with the exception of Samuel Taylor Coleridge, and in a narrower department of thought, with the recent illustrious exception* of David Ricardo),* but also on such a constitution of the *moral* faculties as shall give him an inner eye and power of intuition for the vision and the mysteries of our human nature: *that* constitution of faculties, in short, which (amongst all the generations of men that from the beginning of time have deployed into life, as it were, upon this planet) our English poets have possessed in the highest degree, and Scottish professors* in the lowest.

I have often been asked how I first came to be a regular opium-eater, and have suffered, very unjustly, in the opinion of my acquaintance from being reputed to have brought upon myself all the sufferings which I shall have to record by a long course of indulgence in this practice purely for the sake of creating an artificial state of pleasurable excitement. This, however, is a misrepresentation of my case. True it is that for nearly ten years I did occasionally take opium for the sake of the exquisite pleasure it gave me, but, so long as I took it with this view, I was effectually protected from all material bad consequences by the necessity of interposing long intervals between the several acts of indulgence in order to renew the pleasurable sensations. It was not for the purpose of creating pleasure, but of mitigating pain in the severest degree, that I first began to use opium as an article of daily diet. In the twenty-eighth year of my age, a most painful affection of the stomach, which I had first experienced about ten years before, attacked me in great strength. This affection had originally been caused by extremities of hunger suffered in my boyish days. During the season of hope and redundant happiness which succeeded (that is, from eighteen to twenty-four), it had slumbered; for the three following years it had revived at intervals; and now, under unfavourable circumstances, from depression of spirits, it attacked me with a violence that yielded to no remedies but opium. As the youthful sufferings which first produced this derangement of the stomach were interesting in themselves and in the circumstances that attended them, I shall here briefly retrace them.

My father died when I was about seven years old, and left me to the care of four guardians.* I was sent to various schools, great and small, and was very early distinguished for my classical attainments, especially for my knowledge of Greek. At thirteen, I wrote Greek with ease, and at fifteen my command of that language was so great that I not only composed Greek verses in lyric metres, but could converse in Greek fluently and without embarrassment – an accomplishment which I have not since met with in any scholar of my times, and which, in my case, was owing to the practice of daily reading off the newspapers into the best Greek I could furnish extempore, for the necessity of ransacking my memory and invention for all sorts and combinations of periphrastic expressions as equivalents for modern ideas, images, relations of things, etc., gave me a compass of diction which would never have been called out by a dull translation of moral essays etc. "That boy," said one of my masters,* pointing the attention of a stranger to me, "that boy could harangue an Athenian mob better than you or I could address an English one." He who honoured me with this eulogy was a scholar, "and a ripe and good one",* and of all my tutors was the only one whom I loved or reverenced. Unfortunately for me (and, as I afterwards learnt, to this worthy man's great indignation), I was transferred to the care first of a blockhead,* who was in a perpetual panic lest I should expose his ignorance, and finally to that of a respectable scholar at the head of a great school on an ancient foundation.* This man had been appointed to his situation by —— College, Oxford,* and was a sound, well-built scholar, but (like most men whom I have known from that college) coarse, clumsy and inelegant. A miserable contrast he presented, in my eyes, to the Etonian brilliancy of my favourite master. And besides, he could not disguise from my hourly notice the poverty and meagreness of his understanding. It is a bad thing for a boy to be, and to know himself, far beyond his tutors, whether in knowledge or in power of mind. This was the case so far as regarded knowledge at least, not with myself only, for the two boys who jointly with myself composed the first form were better Grecians than the headmaster, though not more elegant scholars, nor at all more accustomed to sacrifice to the Graces.* When I first entered, I remember that we read Sophocles, and it was a constant matter of triumph to us, the learned triumvirate of the first form, to see our "*archididascalus*"* (as he loved to be called) conning our lesson before we went up and laying a regular train, with lexicon and grammar, for blowing up and blasting (as it were) any difficulties he found in the choruses; whilst *we* never condescended to open our books until the moment of going up, and were generally employed in writing epigrams upon his wig, or some such important matter. My two class fellows were poor and dependant for their future prospects at the university on the recommendation of the headmaster, but I, who had a small patrimonial property, the income of which was sufficient to support me at college, wished to be sent thither immediately. I made earnest representations on the subject to my guardians, but all to no purpose. One, who was more reasonable and had more knowledge of the world than the rest, lived at a distance: two of the other three resigned all their authority into the hands of the fourth, and this fourth, with whom I had to negotiate, was a worthy man in his way, but haughty, obstinate and intolerant of all opposition to his will.* After a certain number of letters and personal interviews, I found that I had nothing to hope for, not even a compromise of the matter, from my guardian: unconditional submission was what he demanded, and I prepared myself, therefore, for other measures. Summer was now coming on with hasty steps, and my seventeenth birthday was fast approaching, after which day I had sworn within myself that I would no longer be numbered amongst schoolboys. Money being what I chiefly wanted, I wrote to a woman of high rank,* who, though young herself, had known me from a child and had latterly treated me with great distinction, requesting that she would "lend" me five guineas. For upwards of a week no answer came, and I was beginning to despond, when, at length, a servant put into my hands a double letter* with a coronet on the seal. The letter was kind and obliging: the fair writer was on the sea coast, and in that way the delay had arisen. She enclosed double of what I had asked and good-naturedly hinted that if I should *never* repay her, it would not absolutely ruin her. Now, then, I was prepared for my scheme: ten guineas, added to about two which I had remaining from my pocket money, seemed to me sufficient for an indefinite length of time – and at that happy age, if no *definite* boundary can be assigned to one's power, the spirit of hope and pleasure makes it virtually infinite.

It is a just remark of Dr Johnson's (and, what cannot often be said of his remarks, it is a very feeling one) that we never do anything consciously for the last time (of things, that is, which we have long been in the habit of doing) without sadness of heart.* This truth I felt deeply when I came to leave ——, a place which I did not love, and where I had not been happy. On the evening before I left —— for ever, I grieved when the ancient and lofty schoolroom resounded with the evening service, performed for the last time in my hearing, and at night, when the muster roll of names was called over, and mine (as usual) was called first, I stepped forward and, passing the headmaster, who was standing by, I bowed to him and looked earnestly in his face, thinking to myself, "He is old and infirm, and in this world I shall not see him again." I was right: I never *did* see him again, nor ever shall. He looked at me complacently, smiled good-naturedly, returned my salutation (or rather, my valediction), and we parted (though he knew it not) for ever. I could not reverence him intellectually, but he had been uniformly kind to me and had allowed me many indulgencies, and I grieved at the thought of the mortification I should inflict upon him.

The morning came which was to launch me into the world, and from which my whole succeeding life has, in many important points, taken its colouring. I lodged in the headmaster's house, and had been allowed, from my first entrance, the indulgence of a private room, which I used both as a sleeping room and as a study. At half after three I rose and gazed with deep emotion at the ancient towers of ——,* "dressed in earliest light"* and beginning to crimson with the radiant lustre of a cloudless July morning. I was firm and immoveable in my purpose, but yet agitated by anticipation of uncertain danger and troubles – and, if I could have foreseen the hurricane and perfect hailstorm of affliction which soon fell upon me, well might I have been agitated. To this agitation the deep peace of the morning presented an affecting contrast, and in some degree a medicine. The silence was more profound than that of midnight, and to me the silence of a summer morning is more touching than all other silence, because, the light being broad and strong, as that of noonday at other seasons of the year, it seems to differ from perfect day, chiefly because man is not yet abroad, and thus the peace of nature and of the innocent creatures of God seems to be secure and deep, only so long as the presence of man, and his restless and unquiet spirit, are not there to trouble its sanctity. I dressed myself, took my hat and gloves, and lingered a little in the room. For the last year and a half this room had been my "pensive citadel":* here I had read and studied through all the hours of night, and though true it was that for the latter part of this time I, who was framed for love and gentle affections, had lost my gaiety and happiness during the strife and fever of contention with my guardian, yet, on the other hand, as a boy so passionately fond of books and dedicated to intellectual pursuits, I could not fail to have enjoyed many happy hours in the midst of general dejection. I wept as I looked round on the chair, hearth, writing table and other familiar objects, knowing too certainly that I looked upon them for the last time. Whilst I write this, it is eighteen years ago, and yet, at this moment, I see distinctly as if it were yesterday the lineaments and expression of the object on which I fixed my parting gaze: it was a picture of the lovely ——,* which hung over the mantelpiece – the eyes and mouth of which were so beautiful, and the whole countenance so radiant with benignity and divine tranquillity, that I had a thousand times laid down my pen or my book to gather consolation from it, as a devotee from his patron saint. Whilst I was yet gazing upon it, the deep tones of —— clock proclaimed that it was four o'clock. I went up to the picture, kissed it and then gently walked out and closed the door for ever!

* * *

So blended and intertwisted in this life are occasions of laughter and of tears that I cannot yet recall without smiling an incident which occurred at that time, and which had nearly put a stop to the immediate execution of my plan. I had a trunk of immense weight, for, besides my clothes, it contained nearly all my library. The difficulty was to get this removed to a carrier's: my room was at an aerial elevation in the house, and (what was worse) the staircase which communicated with this angle of the building was accessible only by a gallery which passed the headmaster's chamber door. I was a favourite with all the servants, and, knowing that any of them would screen me and act confidentially, I communicated my embarrassment to a groom of the headmaster's. The groom swore he would do anything I wished and, when the time arrived, went upstairs to bring the trunk down. This I feared was beyond the strength of any one man; however, the groom was a man

> Of Atlantean shoulders fit to bear
> The weight of mightiest monarchies*

and had a back as spacious as Salisbury Plain. Accordingly, he persisted in bringing down the trunk alone, whilst I stood waiting at the foot of the last flight, in anxiety for the event. For some time I heard him descending with slow and firm steps, but, unfortunately, from his trepidation, as he drew near the dangerous quarter, within a few steps of the gallery, his foot slipped, and the mighty burden, falling from his shoulders, gained such increase of impetus at each step of the descent that, on reaching the bottom, it trundled, or rather leapt, right across, with the noise of twenty devils, against the very bedroom door of the *archididascalus*. My first thought was that all was lost and that my only chance for executing a retreat was to sacrifice my baggage. However, on reflection, I determined to abide the issue. The groom was in the utmost alarm, both on his own account and on mine, but, in spite of this, so irresistibly had the sense of the ludicrous in this unhappy contretemps taken possession of his fancy that he sang out a long, loud and canorous peal of laughter that might have wakened the Seven Sleepers.* At the sound of this resonant merriment within the very ears of insulted authority, I could not myself forbear joining in it: subdued to this not so much by the unhappy *étourderie** of the trunk as by the effect it had upon the groom. We both expected, as a matter of course, that Dr —— would sally out of his room, for, in general, if but a mouse stirred, he sprang out like a mastiff from his kennel. Strange to say, however, on this occasion, when the noise of laughter had ceased, no sound, or rustling even, was to be heard in the bedroom. Dr —— had a painful complaint which, sometimes keeping him awake, made his sleep perhaps, when it *did* come, the deeper. Gathering courage from the silence, the groom hoisted his burden again and accomplished the remainder of his descent without accident. I waited until I saw the trunk placed on a wheelbarrow and on its road to the carrier's, then, "with Providence my guide",* I set off on foot, carrying a small parcel with some articles of dress under my arm, a favourite English poet* in one pocket and a small 12mo* volume containing about nine plays of Euripides in the other.

It had been my intention originally to proceed to Westmorland, both from the love I bore to that county and on other personal accounts.* Accident, however, gave a different direction to my wanderings, and I bent my steps towards North Wales.

After wandering about for some time in Denbighshire, Merionethshire and Caernarvonshire,* I took lodgings in a small neat house in B——.* Here I might have stayed with great comfort for many weeks, for provisions were cheap at B—— from the scarcity of other markets for the surplus produce of a wide agricultural district. An accident, however, in which perhaps no offence was designed, drove me out to wander again. I know not whether my reader may have remarked, but *I* have often remarked that the proudest class of people in England (or, at any rate, the class whose pride is most apparent) are the families of bishops. Noblemen, and their children, carry about with them in their very titles a sufficient notification of their rank. Nay, their very names (and this applies also to the children of many untitled houses) are often, to the English ear, adequate exponents of high birth or descent. Sackville, Manners, Fitzroy, Paulet, Cavendish and scores of others tell their own tale. Such persons, therefore, find everywhere a due sense of their claims already established, except among those who are ignorant of the world by virtue of their own obscurity: "Not to know *them* argues one's self unknown."* Their manners take a suitable tone and colouring, and, for once that they find it necessary to impress a sense of their consequence upon others, they meet with a thousand occasions for moderating and tempering this sense by acts of courteous condescension. With the families of bishops it is otherwise: with them it is all uphill work to make known their pretensions, for the proportion of the episcopal bench taken from noble families is not at any time very large, and the succession to these dignities is so rapid that the public ear seldom has time to become familiar with them, unless where they are connected with some literary reputation. Hence it is that the children of bishops carry about with them an austere and repulsive air indicative of claims not generally acknowledged, a sort of *noli me tangere** manner, nervously apprehensive of too familiar approach and shrinking with the sensitiveness of a gouty man from all contact with the οἱ πολλοί.* Doubtless, a powerful understanding or unusual goodness of nature, will preserve a man from such weakness, but in general the truth of my representation will be acknowledged: pride, if not of deeper root in such families, appears, at least, more upon the surface of their manners. This spirit of manners naturally communicates itself to their domestics and other dependants. Now, my landlady had been a lady's maid or a nurse in the family of the Bishop of ——,* and had but lately married away and "settled" (as such people express it) for life. In a little town like B——, merely to have lived in the bishop's family conferred some distinction, and my good landlady had rather more than her share of the pride I have noticed on that score. What "my lord" said, and what "my lord" did, how useful he was in parliament and how indispensable at Oxford, formed the daily burden of her talk. All this I bore very well, for I was too good-natured to laugh in anybody's face, and I could make an ample allowance for the garrulity of an old servant. Of necessity, however, I must have appeared in her eyes very inadequately impressed with the bishop's importance, and perhaps to punish me for my indifference, or possibly by accident, she one day repeated to me a conversation in which I was indirectly a party concerned. She had been to the palace to pay her respects to the family and, dinner being over, was summoned into the dining room. In giving an account of her household economy, she happened to mention that she had let her apartments. Thereupon the good bishop (it seemed) had taken occasion to caution her as to her selection of inmates: "For," said he, "you must recollect, Betty, that this place is in the high road to the Head,* so that multitudes of Irish swindlers running away from their debts into England, and of English swindlers running away from their debts to the Isle of Man, are likely to take this place in their route." This advice was certainly not without reasonable grounds, but rather fitted to be stored up for Mrs Betty's private meditations than specially reported to me. What followed, however, was somewhat worse: "Oh, my lord," answered my landlady (according to her own representation of the matter), "I really don't think this young gentleman is a swindler, because—" "You don't *think* me a swindler?" said I, interrupting her in a tumult of indignation. "For the future I shall spare you the trouble of thinking about it." And without delay I prepared for my departure. Some concessions the good woman seemed disposed to make, but a harsh and contemptuous expression which I fear that I applied to the learned dignitary himself roused *her* indignation in turn, and reconciliation then became impossible. I was, indeed, greatly irritated at the bishop's having suggested any grounds of suspicion, however remotely, against a person whom he had never seen, and I thought of letting him know my mind in Greek, which at the same time that it would furnish some presumption that I was no swindler would also (I hoped) compel the bishop to reply in the same language, in which case I doubted not to make it appear that if I was not so rich as His Lordship, I was a far better Grecian. Calmer thoughts, however, drove this boyish design out of my mind, for I considered that the bishop was in the right to counsel an old servant; that he could not have designed that his advice should be reported to me; and that the same coarseness of mind which had led Mrs Betty to repeat the advice at all might have coloured it in a way more agreeable to her own style of thinking than to the actual expressions of the worthy bishop.

I left the lodgings the very same hour, and this turned out a very unfortunate occurrence for me, because, living henceforward at inns, I was drained of my money very rapidly. In a fortnight I was reduced to short allowance – that is, I could allow myself only one meal a day. From the keen appetite produced by constant exercise and mountain air acting on a youthful stomach, I soon began to suffer greatly on this slender regimen, for the single meal which I could venture to order was coffee or tea. Even this, however, was at length withdrawn, and afterwards, so long as I remained in Wales, I subsisted either on blackberries, hips, haws,* etc., or on the casual hospitalities which I now and then received in return for such little services as I had an opportunity of rendering. Sometimes I wrote letters of business for cottagers who happened to have relatives in Liverpool or in London; more often I wrote love letters to their sweethearts for young women who had lived as servants in Shrewsbury or other towns on the English border. On all such occasions I gave great satisfaction to my humble friends and was generally treated with hospitality, and once, in particular, near the village of Llan-y-styndw (or some such name),* in a sequestered part of Merionethshire, I was entertained for upwards of three days by a family of young people, with an affectionate and fraternal kindness that left an impression upon my heart not yet impaired. The family consisted, at that time, of four sisters and three brothers, all grown up, and all remarkable for elegance and delicacy of manners. So much beauty, and so much native good breeding and refinement, I do not remember to have seen before or since in any cottage, except once or twice in Westmorland and Devonshire. They spoke English – an accomplishment not often met with in so many members of one family, especially in villages remote from the high road. Here I wrote, on my first introduction, a letter about prize money for one of the brothers, who had served on board an English man-of-war, and, more privately, two love letters for two of the sisters. They were both interesting-looking girls, and one of uncommon loveliness. In the midst of their confusion and blushes whilst dictating, or rather giving me general instructions, it did not require any great penetration to discover that what they wished was that their letters should be as kind as was consistent with proper maidenly pride. I contrived so to temper my expressions as to reconcile the gratification of both feelings, and they were as much pleased with the way in which I had expressed their thoughts as (in their simplicity) they were astonished at my having so readily discovered them. The reception one meets with from the women of a family generally determines the tenor of one's whole entertainment. In this case, I had discharged my confidential duties as secretary so much to the general satisfaction, perhaps also amusing them with my conversation, that I was pressed to stay with a cordiality which I had little inclination to resist. I slept with the brothers, the only unoccupied bed standing in the apartment of the young women, but in all other points they treated me with a respect not usually paid to purses as light as mine, as if my scholarship were sufficient evidence that I was of "gentle blood".* Thus I lived with them for three days and great part of a fourth, and, from the undiminished kindness which they continued to show me, I believe I might have stayed with them up to this time if their power had corresponded with their wishes. On the last morning, however, I perceived upon their countenances, as they sat at breakfast, the expression of some unpleasant communication which was at hand, and soon after one of the brothers explained to me that their parents had gone, the day before my arrival, to an annual meeting of Methodists held at Caernarvon, and were that day expected to return. And if they should not be so civil as they ought to be, he begged, on the part of all the young people, that I would not take it amiss. The parents returned, with churlish faces, and "*Dym Sassenach*" ("No English") in answer to all my addresses. I saw how matters stood, and so, taking an affectionate leave of my kind and interesting young hosts, I went my way. For though they spoke warmly to their parents in my behalf, and often excused the manner of the old people by saying that it was "only their way", yet I easily understood that my talent for writing love letters would do as little to recommend me with two grave sexagenarian Welsh Methodists as my Greek sapphics or alcaics,* and what had been hospitality when offered to me with the gracious courtesy of my young friends would become charity when connected with the harsh demeanour of these old people. Certainly Mr Shelley is right in his notions about old age:* unless powerfully counteracted by all sorts of opposite agencies, it is a miserable corrupter and blighter to the genial charities of the human heart.

Soon after this, I contrived, by means which I must omit for want of room, to transfer myself to London. And now began the latter and fiercer stage of my long sufferings: without using a disproportionate expression, I might say of my agony. For I now suffered, for upwards of sixteen weeks, the physical anguish of hunger in various degrees of intensity, but as bitter, perhaps, as ever any human being can have suffered who has survived it. I would not needlessly harass my reader's feelings by a detail of all that I endured, for extremities such as these, under any circumstances of heaviest misconduct or guilt, cannot be contemplated, even in description, without a rueful pity that is painful to the natural goodness of the human heart. Let it suffice, at least on this occasion, to say that a few fragments of bread from the breakfast table of one individual (who supposed me to be ill, but did not know of my being in utter want), and these at uncertain intervals, constituted my whole support. During the former part of my sufferings (that is, generally in Wales, and always for the first two months in London), I was houseless, and very seldom slept under a roof. To this constant exposure to the open air I ascribe it mainly that I did not sink under my torments. Latterly, however, when colder and more inclement weather came on, and when, from the length of my sufferings, I had begun to sink into a more languishing condition, it was no doubt fortunate for me that the same person to whose breakfast table I had access allowed me to sleep in a large unoccupied house of which he was tenant. "Unoccupied" I call it, for there was no household or establishment in it, nor any furniture, indeed, except a table and a few chairs. But I found, on taking possession of my new quarters, that the house already contained one single inmate: a poor, friendless child, apparently ten years old – but she seemed hunger-bitten,* and sufferings of that sort often make children look older than they are. From this forlorn child I learnt that she had slept and lived there alone for some time before I came, and great joy the poor creature expressed when she found that I was, in future, to be her companion through the hours of darkness. The house was large, and, from the want of furniture, the noise of the rats made a prodigious echoing on the spacious staircase and hall – and, amidst the real fleshly ills of cold and, I fear, hunger, the forsaken child had found leisure to suffer still more (it appeared) from the self-created one of ghosts. I promised her protection against all ghosts whatsoever, but, alas, I could offer her no other assistance. We lay upon the floor with a bundle of cursed law papers for a pillow, but with no other covering than a sort of large horseman's cloak. Afterwards, however, we discovered in a garret an old sofa cover, a small piece of rug and some fragments of other articles which added a little to our warmth. The poor child crept close to me for warmth and for security against her ghostly enemies. When I was not more than usually ill, I took her into my arms, so that in general she was tolerably warm, and often slept when I could not, for during the last two months of my sufferings I slept much in the daytime and was apt to fall into transient dozings at all hours. But my sleep distressed me more than my watching, for, besides the tumultuousness of my dreams (which were only not so awful as those which I shall have to describe hereafter as produced by opium), my sleep was never more than what is called *dog sleep*, so that I could hear myself moaning and was often, as it seemed to me, wakened suddenly by my own voice. And, about this time, a hideous sensation began to haunt me as soon as I fell into a slumber, which has since returned upon me, at different periods of my life, viz. a sort of twitching (I know not where, but apparently about the region of the stomach), which compelled me violently to throw out my feet for the sake of relieving it. This sensation coming on as soon as I began to sleep, and the effort to relieve it constantly awaking me, at length I slept only from exhaustion; and from increasing weakness (as I said before) I was constantly falling asleep and constantly awaking. Meantime, the master of the house sometimes came in upon us suddenly, and very early, sometimes not till ten o'clock, sometimes not at all. He was in constant fear of bailiffs: improving on the plan of Cromwell,* every night he slept in a different quarter of London, and I observed that he never failed to examine, through a private window, the appearance of those who knocked at the door before he would allow it to be opened. He breakfasted alone: indeed, his tea equipage would hardly have admitted of his hazarding an invitation to a second person – any more than the quantity of esculent *matériel*,* which, for the most part, was little more than a roll or a few biscuits which he had bought on his road from the place where he had slept. Or, if he *had* asked a party, as I once learnedly and facetiously observed to him, the several members of it must have *stood* in the relation to each other (not *sat* in any relation whatever) of succession, as the metaphysicians have it, and not of coexistence – in the relation of the parts of time, and not of the parts of space. During his breakfast, I generally contrived a reason for lounging in and, with an air of as much indifference as I could assume, took up such fragments as he had left – sometimes, indeed, there were none at all. In doing this, I committed no robbery except upon the man himself, who was thus obliged (I believe) now and then to send out at noon for an extra biscuit – for, as to the poor child, *she* was never admitted into his study (if I may give that name to his chief depository of parchments, law writings, etc.): that room was to her the Bluebeard room* of the house, being regularly locked on his departure to dinner, about six o'clock, which usually was his final departure for the night. Whether this child were an illegitimate daughter of Mr —— or only a servant, I could not ascertain: she did not herself know, but certainly she was treated altogether as a menial servant. No sooner did Mr —— make his appearance than she went below stairs, brushed his shoes, coat, etc., and, except when she was summoned to run an errand, she never emerged from the dismal Tartarus* of the kitchens etc. to the upper air until my welcome knock at night called up her little trembling footsteps to the front door. Of her life during the daytime, however, I knew little but what I gathered from her own account at night, for, as soon as the hours of business commenced, I saw that my absence would be acceptable – and in general, therefore, I went off and sat in the parks or elsewhere until nightfall.

But who and what, meantime, was the master of the house himself? Reader, he was one of those anomalous practitioners in lower departments of the law who – what shall I say? – who, on prudential reasons or from necessity deny themselves all indulgence in the luxury of too delicate a conscience (a periphrasis which might be abridged considerably, but *that* I leave to the reader's taste). In many walks of life a conscience is a more expensive encumbrance than a wife or a carriage, and just as people talk of "laying down"* their carriages, so I suppose my friend Mr —— had "laid down" his conscience for a time – meaning, doubtless, to resume it as soon as he could afford it. The inner economy of such a man's daily life would present a most strange picture if I could allow myself to amuse the reader at his expense. Even with my limited opportunities for observing what went on, I saw many scenes of London intrigues and complex chicanery, "cycle and epicycle, orb in orb",* at which I sometimes smile to this day – and at which I smiled then, in spite of my misery. My situation, however, at that time gave me little experience, in my own person, of any qualities in Mr ——'s character but such as did him honour. And of his whole strange composition, I must forget everything but that towards me he was obliging and, to the extent of his power, generous.

That power was not, indeed, very extensive; however, in common with the rats, I sat rent-free. And as Dr Johnson has recorded that he never but once in his life had as much wall-fruit as he could eat,* so let me be grateful that on that single occasion I had as large a choice of apartments in a London mansion as I could possibly desire. Except the Bluebeard room, which the poor child believed to be haunted, all others, from the attics to the cellars, were at our service: "the world was all before us",* and we pitched our tent for the night in any spot we chose. This house I have already described as a large one: it stands in a conspicuous situation and in a well-known part of London.* Many of my readers will have passed it, I doubt not, within a few hours of reading this. For myself, I never fail to visit it when business draws me to London. About ten o'clock, this very night, August 15, 1821, being my birthday, I turned aside from my evening walk, down Oxford Street, purposely to take a glance at it: it is now occupied by a respectable family, and, by the lights in the front drawing room, I observed a domestic party, assembled perhaps at tea, and apparently cheerful and gay. Marvellous contrast in my eyes to the darkness, cold, silence and desolation of that same house eighteen years ago, when its nightly occupants were one famishing scholar and a neglected child. Her, by the by, in after years I vainly endeavoured to trace. Apart from her situation, she was not what would be called an interesting child: she was neither pretty, nor quick in understanding, nor remarkably pleasing in manners, but, thank God, even in those years I needed not the embellishments of novel accessories to conciliate my affections – plain human nature, in its humblest and most homely apparel, was enough for me, and I loved the child because she was my partner in wretchedness. If she is now living, she is probably a mother, with children of her own, but, as I have said, I could never trace her.

This I regret, but another person there was at that time whom I have since sought to trace with far deeper earnestness and with far deeper sorrow at my failure. This person was a young woman, and one of that unhappy class who subsist upon the wages of prostitution. I feel no shame, nor have any reason to feel it, in avowing that I was then on familiar and friendly terms with many women in that unfortunate condition. The reader needs neither smile at this avowal nor frown. For, not to remind my classical readers of the old Latin proverb "*Sine Cerere*"* etc., it may well be supposed that in the existing state of my purse, my connection with such women could not have been an impure one. But the truth is that at no time of my life have I been a person to hold myself polluted by the touch or approach of any creature that wore a human shape: on the contrary, from my very earliest youth it has been my pride to converse familiarly, *more Socratico*,* with all human beings – man, woman and child – that chance might fling in my way – a practice which is friendly to the knowledge of human nature, to good feelings and to that frankness of address which becomes a man who would be thought a philosopher. For a philosopher should not see with the eyes of the poor limitary creature, calling himself a man of the world, and filled with narrow and self-regarding prejudices of birth and education, but should look upon himself as a catholic* creature, and as standing in an equal relation to high and low, to educated and uneducated, to the guilty and the innocent. Being myself at that time of necessity a peripatetic, or a walker of the streets, I naturally fell in more frequently with those female peripatetics who are technically called streetwalkers. Many of these women had occasionally taken my part against watchmen who wished to drive me off the steps of houses where I was sitting. But one amongst them, the one on whose account I have at all introduced this subject – yet no! let me not class thee, O noble-minded Ann ——, with that order of women, let me find, if it be possible, some gentler name to designate the condition of her to whose bounty and compassion, ministering to my necessities when all the world had forsaken me, I owe it that I am at this time alive. For many weeks I had walked at nights with this poor friendless girl up and down Oxford Street, or had rested with her on steps and under the shelter of porticoes. She could not be so old as myself: she told me, indeed, that she had not completed her sixteenth year. By such questions as my interest about her prompted, I had gradually drawn forth her simple history. Hers was a case of ordinary occurrence (as I have since had reason to think), and one in which, if London beneficence had better adapted its arrangements to meet it, the power of the law might oftener be interposed to protect and to avenge. But the stream of London charity flows in a channel which, though deep and mighty, is yet noiseless and underground – not obvious or readily accessible to poor houseless wanderers – and it cannot be denied that the outside air and framework of London society is harsh, cruel and repulsive. In any case, however, I saw that part of her injuries might easily have been redressed, and I urged her often and earnestly to lay her complaint before a magistrate. Friendless as she was, I assured her that she would meet with immediate attention, and that English justice, which was no respecter of persons, would speedily and amply avenge her on the brutal ruffian who had plundered her little property. She promised me often that she would, but she delayed taking the steps I pointed out from time to time, for she was timid and dejected to a degree which showed how deeply sorrow had taken hold of her young heart, and perhaps she thought justly that the most upright judge and the most righteous tribunals could do nothing to repair her heaviest wrongs. Something, however, would perhaps have been done, for it had been settled between us at length, but unhappily on the very last time but one that I was ever to see her, that in a day or two we should go together before a magistrate and that I should speak on her behalf. This little service it was destined, however, that I should never realize. Meantime, that which she rendered to me, and which was greater than I could ever have repaid her, was this: one night, when we were pacing slowly along Oxford Street, and after a day when I had felt more than usually ill and faint, I requested her to turn off with me into Soho Square. Thither we went, and we sat down on the steps of a house – which, to this hour, I never pass without a pang of grief and an inner act of homage to the spirit of that unhappy girl, in memory of the noble action which she there performed. Suddenly, as we sat, I grew much worse. I had been leaning my head against her bosom, and all at once I sank from her arms and fell backwards on the steps. From the sensations I then had, I felt an inner conviction of the liveliest kind that without some powerful and reviving stimulus I should either have died on the spot or should at least have sunk to a point of exhaustion from which all reascent under my friendless circumstances would soon have become hopeless. Then it was, at this crisis of my fate, that my poor orphan companion – who had herself met with little but injuries in this world – stretched out a saving hand to me. Uttering a cry of terror, but without a moment's delay, she ran off into Oxford Street and, in less time than could be imagined, returned to me with a glass of port wine and spices that acted upon my empty stomach (which at that time would have rejected all solid food) with an instantaneous power of restoration. And for this glass the generous girl without a murmur paid out of her own humble purse at a time – be it remembered! – when she had scarcely wherewithal to purchase the bare necessaries of life, and when she could have no reason to expect that I should ever be able to reimburse her. Oh, youthful benefactress! How often in succeeding years, standing in solitary places and thinking of thee with grief of heart and perfect love, how often have I wished that, as in ancient times the curse of a father was believed to have a supernatural power and to pursue its object with a fatal necessity of self-fulfilment, even so the benediction of a heart oppressed with gratitude might have a like prerogative – might have power given to it from above to chase, to haunt, to waylay,* to overtake, to pursue thee into the central darkness of a London brothel, or (if it were possible) into the darkness of the grave, there to awaken thee with an authentic message of peace and forgiveness, and of final reconciliation!

I do not often weep, for not only do my thoughts on subjects connected with the chief interests of man daily, nay hourly, descend a thousand fathoms "too deep for tears"* – not only does the sternness of my habits of thought present an antagonism to the feelings which prompt tears, wanting of necessity to those who, being protected usually by their levity from any tendency to meditative sorrow, would by that same levity be made incapable of resisting it on any casual access of such feelings – but also I believe that all minds which have contemplated such objects as deeply as I have done must, for their own protection from utter despondency, have early encouraged and cherished some tranquillizing belief as to the future balances and the hieroglyphic meanings of human sufferings. On these accounts, I am cheerful to this hour – and, as I have said, I do not often weep. Yet some feelings, though not deeper or more passionate, are more tender than others, and often, when I walk at this time in Oxford Street by dreamy lamplight and hear those airs played on a barrel organ which years ago solaced me and my dear companion (as I must always call her), I shed tears and muse with myself at the mysterious dispensation which so suddenly and so critically separated us for ever. How it happened, the reader will understand from what remains of this introductory narration.

Soon after the period of the last incident I have recorded, I met, in Albemarle Street, a gentleman of His late Majesty's* household. This gentleman had received hospitalities, on different occasions, from my family, and he challenged me upon the strength of my family likeness. I did not attempt any disguise: I answered his questions ingenuously, and, on his pledging his word of honour that he would not betray me to my guardians, I gave him an address to my friend the attorney's. The next day I received from him a 10*l.** banknote. The letter enclosing it was delivered with other letters of business to the attorney, but, though his look and manner informed me that he suspected its contents, he gave it up to me honourably and without demur.

This present, from the particular service to which it was applied, leads me naturally to speak of the purpose which had allured me up to London, and which I had been (to use a forensic word) *soliciting* from the first day of my arrival in London to that of my final departure.

In so mighty a world as London, it will surprise my readers that I should not have found some means of staving off the last extremities of penury, and it will strike them that two resources at least must have been open to me, viz. either to seek assistance from the friends of my family or to turn my youthful talents and attainments into some channel of pecuniary emolument. As to the first course, I may observe, generally, that what I dreaded beyond all other evils was the chance of being reclaimed by my guardians, not doubting that whatever power the law gave them would have been enforced against me to the utmost – that is, to the extremity of forcibly restoring me to the school which I had quitted: a restoration which, as it would in my eyes have been a dishonour, even if submitted to voluntarily, could not fail, when extorted from me in contempt and defiance of my known wishes and efforts, to have been a humiliation worse to me than death, and which would indeed have terminated in death. I was, therefore, shy enough of applying for assistance even in those quarters where I was sure of receiving it, at the risk of furnishing my guardians with any clue for recovering me. But, as to London in particular, though doubtless my father had in his lifetime had many friends there, yet (as ten years had passed since his death) I remembered few of them even by name, and never having seen London before, except once for a few hours, I knew not the address of even those few. To this mode of gaining help, therefore, in part the difficulty, but much more the paramount fear which I have mentioned, habitually indisposed me. In regard to the other mode, I now feel half inclined to join my reader in wondering that I should have overlooked it. As a corrector of Greek proofs (if in no other way), I might doubtless have gained enough for my slender wants. Such an office as this I could have discharged with an exemplary and punctual accuracy that would soon have gained me the confidence of my employers. But it must not be forgotten that, even for such an office as this, it was necessary that I should first of all have an introduction to some respectable publisher, and this I had no means of obtaining. To say the truth, however, it had never once occurred to me to think of literary labours as a source of profit. No mode sufficiently speedy of obtaining money had ever occurred to me but that of borrowing it on the strength of my future claims and expectations. This mode I sought by every avenue to compass, and amongst other persons I applied to a Jew named D——.*

To this Jew, and to other advertising moneylenders (some of whom were, I believe, also Jews), I had introduced myself with an account of my expectations – which account, on examining my father's will at Doctors' Commons,* they had ascertained to be correct. The person there mentioned as the second son of ——, was found to have all the claims (or more than all) that I had stated. But one question still remained, which the faces of the Jews pretty significantly suggested: was *I* that person? This doubt had never occurred to me as a possible one. I had rather feared, whenever my Jewish friends scrutinized me keenly, that I might be too well known to be that person, and that some scheme might be passing in their minds for entrapping me and selling me to my guardians. It was strange to me to find my own self, *materialiter* considered (so I expressed it, for I doted on logical accuracy of distinctions), accused, or at least suspected, of counterfeiting my own self, *formaliter** considered. However, to satisfy their scruples, I took the only course in my power. Whilst I was in Wales, I had received various letters from young friends: these I produced, for I carried them constantly in my pocket – being, indeed, by this time, almost the only relics of my personal encumbrances (excepting the clothes I wore) which I had not in one way or other disposed of. Most of these letters were from the Earl of ——, who was at that time my chief (or rather only) confidential friend. These letters were dated from Eton. I had also some from the Marquess of ——,* his father, who, though absorbed in agricultural pursuits, yet having been an Etonian himself, and as good a scholar as a nobleman needs to be, still retained an affection for classical studies and for youthful scholars. He had, accordingly, from the time that I was fifteen, corresponded with me – sometimes upon the great improvements which he had made, or was meditating, in the counties of M— and Sl—* since I had been there, sometimes upon the merits of a Latin poet, at other times suggesting subjects to me on which he wished me to write verses.

On reading the letters, one of my Jewish friends agreed to furnish two or three hundred pounds on my personal security, provided I could persuade the young Earl, who was, by the way, not older than myself, to guarantee the payment on our coming of age – the Jew's final object being, as I now suppose, not the trifling profit he could expect to make by me, but the prospect of establishing a connection with my noble friend, whose immense expectations were well known to him. In pursuance of this proposal on the part of the Jew, about eight or nine days after I had received the 10*l.* I prepared to go down to Eton. Nearly 3*l.* of the money I had given to my money-lending friend, on his alleging that the stamps must be bought in order that the writings might be preparing whilst I was away from London. I thought in my heart that he was lying, but I did not wish to give him any excuse for charging his own delays upon me. A smaller sum I had given to my friend the attorney (who was connected with the moneylenders as their lawyer) – to which, indeed, he was entitled for his unfurnished lodgings. About fifteen shillings I had employed in re-establishing (though in a very humble way) my dress. Of the remainder I gave one quarter to Ann, meaning on my return to have divided with her whatever might remain. These arrangements made, soon after six o'clock, on a dark winter evening, I set off, accompanied by Ann, towards Piccadilly, for it was my intention to go down as far as Salt Hill on the Bath or Bristol Mail. Our course lay through a part of the town which has now all disappeared, so that I can no longer retrace its ancient boundaries: Swallow Street, I think it was called. Having time enough before us, however, we bore away to the left until we came into Golden Square. There, near the corner of Sherrard Street, we sat down, not wishing to part in the tumult and blaze of Piccadilly. I had told her of my plans some time before, and I now assured her again that she should share in my good fortune, if I met with any, and that I would never forsake her, as soon as I had power to protect her. This I fully intended, as much from inclination as from a sense of duty, for, setting aside gratitude, which in any case must have made me her debtor for life, I loved her as affectionately as if she had been my sister, and at this moment with sevenfold tenderness from pity at witnessing her extreme dejection. I had, apparently, most reason for dejection, because I was leaving the saviour of my life, yet I, considering the shock my health had received, was cheerful and full of hope. She, on the contrary, who was parting with one who had had little means of serving her except by kindness and brotherly treatment, was overcome by sorrow, so that, when I kissed her at our final farewell, she put her arms about my neck and wept without speaking a word. I hoped to return in a week at furthest, and I agreed with her that on the fifth night from that, and every night afterwards, she should wait for me at six o'clock near the bottom of Great Titchfield Street, which had been our customary haven, as it were, of rendezvous, to prevent our missing each other in the great Mediterranean of Oxford Street. This, and other measures of precaution I took: one only I forgot. She had either never told me, or (as a matter of no great interest) I had forgotten, her surname. It is a general practice, indeed, with girls of humble rank in her unhappy condition not (as novel-reading women of higher pretensions) to style themselves Miss Douglas, Miss Montague, etc., but simply by their Christian names, Mary, Jane, Frances, etc. Her surname, as the surest means of tracing her hereafter, I ought now to have enquired, but the truth is, having no reason to think that our meeting could, in consequence of a short interruption, be more difficult or uncertain than it had been for so many weeks, I had scarcely for a moment adverted to it as necessary, or placed it amongst my memoranda against this parting interview – and, my final anxieties being spent in comforting her with hopes and in pressing upon her the necessity of getting some medicines for a violent cough and hoarseness with which she was troubled, I wholly forgot it until it was too late to recall her.

It was past eight o'clock when I reached the Gloucester Coffee House, and, the Bristol mail being on the point of going off, I mounted on the outside. The fine fluent motion of this mail* soon laid me asleep: it is somewhat remarkable that the first easy or refreshing sleep which I had enjoyed for some months was on the outside of a mail coach – a bed which, at this day, I find rather an uneasy one. Connected with this sleep was a little incident which served, as hundreds of others did at that time, to convince me how easily a man who has never been in any great distress may pass through life without knowing, in his own person at least, anything of the possible goodness of the human heart – or, as I must add with a sigh, of its possible vileness. So thick a curtain of *manners* is drawn over the features and expression of men's *natures* that, to the ordinary observer, the two extremities, and the infinite field of varieties which lie between them, are all confounded – the vast and multitudinous compass of their several harmonies reduced to the meagre outline of differences expressed in the gamut or alphabet of elementary sounds. The case was this: for the first four or five miles from London, I annoyed my fellow passenger on the roof by occasionally falling against him when the coach gave a lurch to his side – and indeed, if the road had been less smooth and level than it is, I should have fallen off from weakness. Of this annoyance he complained heavily, as perhaps in the same circumstances most people would. He expressed his complaint, however, more morosely than the occasion seemed to warrant, and, if I had parted with him at that moment, I should have thought of him (if I had considered it worthwhile to think of him at all) as a surly and almost brutal fellow. However, I was conscious that I had given him some cause for complaint, and therefore I apologized to him and assured him I would do what I could to avoid falling asleep for the future – and, at the same time, in as few words as possible, I explained to him that I was ill and in a weak state from long suffering, and that I could not afford at that time to take an inside place. The man's manner changed, upon hearing this explanation, in an instant, and when I next woke for a minute from the noise and lights of Hounslow (for in spite of my wishes and efforts I had fallen asleep again within two minutes from the time I had spoken to him) I found that he had put his arm round me to protect me from falling off, and for the rest of my journey he behaved to me with the gentleness of a woman, so that, at length, I almost lay in his arms – and this was the more kind as he could not have known that I was not going the whole way to Bath or Bristol. Unfortunately, indeed, I *did* go rather farther than I intended, for so genial and refreshing was my sleep that the next time, after leaving Hounslow, that I fully awoke was upon the sudden pulling up of the mail (possibly at a post office) – and, on enquiry, I found that we had reached Maidenhead – six or seven miles, I think, ahead of Salt Hill. Here I alighted, and for the half-minute that the mail stopped I was entreated by my friendly companion (who, from the transient glimpse I had had of him in Piccadilly, seemed to me to be a gentleman's butler, or person of that rank) to go to bed without delay. This I promised, though with no intention of doing so, and in fact I immediately set forward, or rather backward, on foot. It must then have been nearly midnight, but so slowly did I creep along that I heard a clock in a cottage strike four before I turned down the lane from Slough to Eton. The air and the sleep had both refreshed me, but I was weary nevertheless. I remember a thought (obvious enough, and which has been prettily expressed by a Roman poet)* which gave me some consolation at that moment under my poverty. There had been some time before a murder committed on or near Hounslow Heath. I think I cannot be mistaken when I say that the name of the murdered person was Steele, and that he was the owner of a lavender plantation in that neighbourhood.* Every step of my progress was bringing me nearer to the Heath, and it naturally occurred to me that I and the accursed murderer, if he were that night abroad, might at every instant be unconsciously approaching each other through the darkness. In which case, said I, supposing I, instead of being (as indeed I am) little better than an outcast,

> Lord of my learning and no land beside,*

were, like my friend Lord ——,* heir by general repute to 70,000*l*. per ann., what a panic should I be under at this moment about my throat! Indeed, it was not likely that Lord —— should ever be in my situation. But, nevertheless, the spirit of the remark remains true – that vast power and possessions make a man shamefully afraid of dying – and I am convinced that many of the most intrepid adventurers, who, by fortunately being poor, enjoy the full use of their natural courage, would, if at the very instant of going into action news were brought to them that they had unexpectedly succeeded to an estate in England of 50,000*l*. a year, feel their dislike to bullets considerably sharpened* and their efforts at perfect equanimity and self-possession proportionably difficult. So true it is, in the language of a wise man whose own experience had made him acquainted with both fortunes, that riches are better fitted

> To slacken Virtue and abate her edge
> Than tempt her to do aught may merit praise.*
> *Parad. Regained*

I dally with my subject because, to myself, the remembrance of these times is profoundly interesting. But my reader shall not have any further cause to complain, for I now hasten to its close. In the road between Slough and Eton I fell asleep, and, just as the morning began to dawn, I was awakened by the voice of a man standing over me and surveying me. I know not what he was: he was an ill-looking fellow, but not therefore of necessity an ill-meaning fellow – or, if he were, I suppose he thought that no person sleeping out of doors in winter could be worth robbing. In which conclusion, however, as it regarded myself, I beg to assure him, if he should be among my readers, that he was mistaken. After a slight remark he passed on, and I was not sorry at his disturbance, as it enabled me to pass through Eton before people were generally up. The night had been heavy and louring, but towards the morning it had changed to a slight frost, and the ground and the trees were now covered with rime. I slipped through Eton unobserved, washed myself and, as far as possible, adjusted my dress at a little public house in Windsor, and about eight o'clock went down towards Pote's.* On my road I met some junior boys, of whom I made enquiries: an Etonian is always a gentleman – and, in spite of my shabby habiliments, they answered me civilly. My friend, Lord ——, was gone to the University of ——.* "*Ibi omnis effusus labor!*"* I had, however, other friends at Eton, but it is not to all who wear that name in prosperity that a man is willing to present himself in distress. On recollecting myself, however, I asked for the Earl of D——,* to whom, though my acquaintance with him was not so intimate as with some others, I should not have shrunk from presenting myself under any circumstances. He was still at Eton, though I believe on the wing for Cambridge. I called, was received kindly and asked to breakfast.

Here let me stop for a moment to check my reader from any erroneous conclusions: because I have had occasion incidentally to speak of various patrician friends, it must not be supposed that I have myself any pretensions to rank or high blood. I thank God that I have not. I am the son of a plain English merchant, esteemed during his life for his great integrity, and strongly attached to literary pursuits (indeed, he was himself, anonymously, an author).* If he had lived, it was expected that he would have been very rich, but, dying prematurely, he left no more than about 30,000*l.* amongst seven different claimants. My mother I may mention with honour as still more highly gifted. For, though unpretending to the name and honours of a *literary* woman, I shall presume to call her (what many literary women are not) an *intellectual* woman, and I believe that if ever her letters should be collected and published, they would be thought generally to exhibit as much strong and masculine sense, delivered in as pure "mother English",* racy and fresh with idiomatic graces, as any in our language – hardly excepting those of Lady M.W. Montagu.* These are my honours of descent: I have no others, and I have thanked God sincerely that I have not, because, in my judgement, a station which raises a man too eminently above the level of his fellow creatures is not the most favourable to moral or to intellectual qualities.

Lord D—— placed before me a most magnificent breakfast. It was really so, but in my eyes it seemed trebly magnificent from being the first regular meal, the first "good man's table",* that I had sat down to for months. Strange to say, however, I could scarcely eat anything. On the day when I first received my 10*l.* banknote, I had gone to a baker's shop and bought a couple of rolls. This very shop I had two months or six weeks before surveyed with an eagerness of desire which it was almost humiliating to me to recollect. I remembered the story about Otway* and feared that there might be danger in eating too rapidly. But I had no need for alarm: my appetite was quite sunk, and I became sick before I had eaten half of what I had bought. This effect from eating what approached to a meal I continued to feel for weeks – or, when I did not experience any nausea, part of what I ate was rejected, sometimes with acidity, sometimes immediately and without any acidity. On the present occasion, at Lord D——'s table, I found myself not at all better than usual, and, in the midst of luxuries, I had no appetite. I had however, unfortunately, at all times a craving for wine. I explained my situation, therefore, to Lord D——, and gave him a short account of my late sufferings, at which he expressed great compassion and called for wine. This gave me a momentary relief and pleasure, and on all occasions when I had an opportunity I never failed to drink wine, which I worshipped then as I have since worshipped opium. I am convinced, however, that this indulgence in wine contributed to strengthen my malady, for the tone of my stomach was apparently quite sunk, but by a better regimen it might sooner, and perhaps effectually, have been revived. I hope that it was not from this love of wine that I lingered in the neighbourhood of my Eton friends. I persuaded myself *then* that it was from reluctance to ask of Lord D——, on whom I was conscious I had not sufficient claims, the particular service in quest of which I had come down to Eton. I was, however, unwilling to lose my journey, and... I asked it. Lord D——, whose good nature was unbounded, and which, in regard to myself, had been measured rather by his compassion perhaps for my condition and his knowledge of my intimacy with some of his relatives* than by an over-rigorous enquiry into the extent of my own direct claims, faltered, nevertheless, at this request. He acknowledged that he did not like to have any dealings with moneylenders, and feared lest such a transaction might come to the ears of his connections. Moreover, he doubted whether *his* signature, whose expectations were so much more bounded than those of ——, would avail with my unchristian friends. However, he did not wish, as it seemed, to mortify me by an absolute refusal, for, after a little consideration, he promised, under certain conditions which he pointed out, to give his security. Lord D—— was at this time not eighteen years of age, but I have often doubted, on recollecting since the good sense and prudence which on this occasion he mingled with so much urbanity of manner (an urbanity which in him wore the grace of youthful sincerity), whether any statesman – the oldest and the most accomplished in diplomacy – could have acquitted himself better under the same circumstances. Most people, indeed, cannot be addressed on such a business without surveying you with looks as austere and unpropitious as those of a Saracen's head.

Recomforted by this promise, which was not quite equal to the best, but far above the worst that I had pictured to myself as possible, I returned in a Windsor coach to

London three days after I had quitted it. And now I come to the end of my story: the Jews did not approve of Lord D——'s terms. Whether they would in the end have acceded to them and were only seeking time for making due enquiries, I know not, but many delays were made, time passed on, the small fragment of my banknote had just melted away, and before any conclusion could have been put to the business, I must have relapsed into my former state of wretchedness. Suddenly, however, at this crisis, an opening was made, almost by accident, for reconciliation with my friends. I quitted London, in haste, for a remote part of England. After some time, I proceeded to the university, and it was not until many months had passed away that I had it in my power again to revisit the ground which had become so interesting to me, and to this day remains so, as the chief scene of my youthful sufferings.

Meantime, what had become of poor Ann? For her I have reserved my concluding words. According to our agreement, I sought her daily, and waited for her every night, so long as I stayed in London, at the corner of Titchfield Street. I enquired for her of everyone who was likely to know her, and, during the last hours of my stay in London, I put into activity every means of tracing her that my knowledge of London suggested and the limited extent of my power made possible. The street where she had lodged I knew, but not the house, and I remembered at last some account which she had given me of ill-treatment from her landlord, which made it probable that she had quitted those lodgings before we parted. She had few acquaintance; most people, besides, thought that the earnestness of my enquiries arose from motives which moved their laughter or their slight regard, and others, thinking I was in chase of a girl who had robbed me of some trifles, were naturally and excusably indisposed to give me any clue to her – if, indeed, they had any to give. Finally, as my despairing resource, on the day I left London I put into the hands of the only person who (I was sure) must know Ann by sight, from having been in company with us once or twice, an address to —— in ——shire,* at that time the residence of my family. But, to this hour, I have never heard a syllable about her. This, amongst such troubles as most men meet with in this life, has been my heaviest affliction. If she lived, doubtless we must have been sometimes in search of each other at the very same moment through the mighty labyrinths of London – perhaps even within a few feet of each other, a barrier no wider in a London street, often amounting in the end to a separation for eternity! During some years, I hoped that she *did* live, and I suppose that, in the literal and unrhetorical use of the word *myriad*,* I may say that on my different visits to London I have looked into many, many myriads of female faces in the hope of meeting her. I should know her again amongst a thousand, if I saw her for a moment, for though not handsome, she had a sweet expression of countenance and a peculiar and graceful carriage of the head. I sought her, I have said, in hope. So it was for years, but now I should fear to see her – and her cough, which grieved me when I parted with her, is now my consolation. I now wish to see her no longer, but think of her, more gladly, as one long since laid in the grave – in the grave, I would hope, of a magdalen,* taken away before injuries and cruelty had blotted out and transfigured her ingenuous nature, or the brutalities of ruffians had completed the ruin they had begun.

PART II

SO THEN, OXFORD STREET, stony-hearted stepmother, thou that listenest to the sighs of orphans and drinkest the tears of children, at length I was dismissed from thee! The time was come at last that I no more should pace in anguish thy never-ending terraces – no more should dream and wake in captivity to the pangs of hunger. Successors, too many, to myself and Ann have doubtless since then trodden in our footsteps – inheritors of our calamities. Other orphans than Ann have sighed, tears have been shed by other children, and thou, Oxford Street, hast since, doubtless, echoed to the groans of innumerable hearts. For myself, however, the storm which I had outlived seemed to have been the pledge of a long fair weather – the premature sufferings which I had paid down, to have been accepted as a ransom for many years to come as a price of long immunity from sorrow – and if again I walked in London, a solitary and contemplative man (as oftentimes I did), I walked for the most part in serenity and peace of mind. And, although it is true that the calamities of my novitiate in London had struck root so deeply in my bodily constitution that afterwards they shot up and flourished afresh and grew into a noxious umbrage that has overshadowed and darkened my latter years, yet these second assaults of suffering were met with a fortitude more confirmed, with the resources of a maturer intellect and with alleviations from sympathizing affection – how deep and tender!

Thus, however, with whatsoever alleviations, years that were far asunder were bound together by subtle links of suffering derived from a common root. And herein I notice an instance of the short-sightedness of human desires: that oftentimes on moonlight nights, during my first mournful abode in London, my consolation was (if such it could be thought) to gaze from Oxford Street up every avenue in succession which pierces through the heart of Marylebone to the fields and the woods. "For *that*," said I, travelling with my eyes up the long vistas which lay part in light and part in shade, "*that* is the road to the north, and therefore to ——, and if I had the wings of a dove, *that* way I would fly for comfort."* Thus I said, and thus I wished, in my blindness, yet even in that very northern region it was, even in that very valley – nay, in that very house to which my erroneous wishes pointed – that this second birth of my sufferings began, and that they again threatened to besiege the citadel of life and hope. There it was that for years I was persecuted by visions as ugly and as ghastly phantoms as ever haunted the couch of an Orestes* – and in this unhappier than he: that sleep, which comes to all as a respite and a restoration, and to him especially as a blessed* balm for his wounded heart and his haunted brain, visited me as my bitterest scourge. Thus blind was I in my desires, yet if a veil interposes between the dim-sightedness of man and his future calamities, the same veil hides from him their alleviations, and a grief which had not been feared is met by consolations which had not been hoped. I, therefore, who participated, as it were, in the troubles of Orestes (excepting only in his agitated conscience), participated no less in all his supports: my Eumenides, like his, were at my bed feet, and stared in upon me through the curtains, but, watching by my pillow, or defrauding herself of sleep to bear me company through the heavy watches of the night, sat my Electra – for thou, beloved M.,* dear companion of my later years, thou wast my Electra, and neither in nobility of mind nor in long-suffering affection wouldst permit that a Grecian sister should excel an English wife! For thou thoughtest not much to stoop to humble offices of kindness and to servile* ministrations of tenderest affection, to wipe away for years the unwholesome dews upon the forehead, or to refresh the lips when parched and baked with fever – nor even when thy own peaceful slumbers had by long sympathy become infected with the spectacle of my dread contest with phantoms and shadowy enemies that oftentimes bade me "sleep no more!" – not even then didst thou utter a complaint or any murmur, nor withdraw thy angelic smiles, nor shrink from thy service of love more than Electra did of old. For she too, though she was a Grecian woman and the daughter of the king of men,* yet wept sometimes and hid her face* in her robe.

But these troubles are past, and thou wilt read these records of a period so dolorous to us both as the legend of some hideous dream that can return no more. Meantime, I am again in London, and again I pace the terraces of Oxford Street by night. And oftentimes, when I am oppressed by anxieties that demand all my philosophy and the comfort of thy presence to support, and yet remember that I am separated from thee by three hundred miles and the length of three dreary months, I look up the streets that run northwards from Oxford Street, upon moonlight nights, and recollect my youthful ejaculation of anguish. And remembering that thou art sitting alone in that same valley, and mistress of that very house to which my heart turned in its blindness nineteen years ago, I think that, though blind indeed and scattered to the winds of late, the promptings of my heart may yet have had reference to a remoter time and may be justified if read in another meaning – and, if I could allow myself to descend again to the impotent wishes of childhood, I should again say to myself, as I look to the north, "Oh, that I had the wings of a dove...", and with how just a confidence in thy good and gracious nature might I add the other half of my early ejaculation: "And *that* way I would fly for comfort."

THE PLEASURES OF OPIUM

IT IS SO LONG SINCE I FIRST TOOK opium that if it had been a trifling incident in my life, I might have forgotten its date. But cardinal events are not to be forgotten, and from circumstances connected with it, I remember that it must be referred to the autumn of 1804. During that season I was in London, having come thither for the first time since my entrance at college.* And my introduction to opium arose in the following way. From an early age I had been accustomed to wash my head in cold water at least once a day. Being suddenly seized with toothache, I attributed it to some relaxation caused by an accidental intermission of that practice – jumped out of bed, plunged my head into a basin of cold water and with hair thus wetted went to sleep. The next morning, as I need hardly say, I awoke with excruciating rheumatic pains of the head and face, from which I had hardly any respite for about twenty days. On the twenty-first day, I think it was, and on a Sunday, that I went out into the streets – rather to run away, if possible, from my torments than with any distinct purpose. By accident I met a college acquaintance who recommended opium. Opium! Dread agent of unimaginable pleasure and pain! I had heard of it as I had of manna or of ambrosia, but no further. How unmeaning a sound was it at that time! What solemn chords does it now strike upon my heart! What heart-quaking vibrations of sad and happy remembrances! Reverting for a moment to these, I feel a mystic importance attached to the minutest circumstances connected with the place and the time and the man (if man he was) that first laid open to me the paradise of opium-eaters. It was a Sunday afternoon, wet and cheerless, and a duller spectacle this earth of ours has not to show* than a rainy Sunday in London. My road homewards lay through Oxford Street, and near "the *stately* Pantheon"* (as Mr Wordsworth has obligingly called it) I saw a druggist's shop. The druggist – unconscious minister of celestial pleasures! – as if in sympathy with the rainy Sunday, looked dull and stupid, just as any mortal druggist might be expected to look on a Sunday. And when I asked for the tincture of opium, he gave it to me as any other man might do. And, furthermore, out of my shilling returned me what seemed to be real copper halfpence, taken out of a real wooden drawer. Nevertheless, in spite of such indications of humanity, he has ever since existed in my mind as the beatific vision of an immortal druggist sent down to earth on a special mission to myself. And it confirms me in this way of considering him that when I next came up to London, I sought him near the stately Pantheon and found him not. And thus to me, who knew not his name (if indeed he had one), he seemed rather to have vanished from Oxford Street than to have removed in any bodily fashion. The reader may choose to think of him as, possibly, no more than a sublunary druggist. It may be so, but my faith is better: I believe him to have evanesced* or evaporated. So unwillingly would I connect any mortal remembrances with that hour and place and creature that first brought me acquainted with the celestial drug.

Arrived at my lodgings, it may be supposed that I lost not a moment in taking the quantity prescribed. I was necessarily ignorant of the whole art and mystery of opium-taking, and what I took, I took under every disadvantage. But I took it, and in an hour, oh, Heavens, what a revulsion!* What an upheaving, from its lowest depths, of the inner spirit! What an apocalypse of the world within me! That my pains had vanished was now a trifle in my eyes: this negative effect was swallowed up in the immensity of those positive effects which had opened before me – in the abyss of divine enjoyment thus suddenly revealed. Here was a panacea – a φάρμακον νηπενθές* for all human woes. Here was the secret of happiness, about which philosophers had disputed for so many ages, at once discovered. Happiness might now be bought for a penny and carried in the waistcoat pocket. Portable ecstasies might be had corked up in a pint bottle, and peace of mind could be sent down in gallons by the mail coach. But if I talk in this way, the reader will think I am laughing, and I can assure him that nobody will laugh long who deals much with opium: its pleasures even are of a grave and solemn complexion, and in his happiest state the opium-eater cannot present himself in the character of 'L'Allegro' – even then he speaks and thinks as becomes 'Il Penseroso'.* Nevertheless, I have a very reprehensible way of jesting at times in the midst of my own misery – and, unless when I am checked by some more powerful feelings, I am afraid I shall be guilty of this indecent practice even in these annals of suffering or enjoyment. The reader must allow a little to my infirm nature in this respect, and with a few indulgences of that sort I shall endeavour to be as grave, if not drowsy, as fits a theme like opium, so anti-mercurial as it really is and so drowsy as it is falsely reputed.

And, first, one word with respect to its bodily effects: for upon all that has been hitherto written on the subject of opium, whether by travellers in Turkey (who may plead their privilege of lying as an old immemorial right) or by professors of medicine writing *ex cathedra*,* I have but one emphatic criticism to pronounce: "Lies! Lies! Lies!" I remember once, in passing a bookstall, to have caught these words from a page of some satiric author:* "By this time I became convinced that the London newspapers spoke truth at least twice a week, viz. on Tuesday and Saturday, and might safely be depended upon for... the list of bankrupts."* In like manner, I do by no means deny that some truths have been delivered to the world in regard to opium. Thus it has been repeatedly affirmed by the learned that opium is a dusky brown in colour – and this, take notice, I grant. Secondly, that it is rather dear, which also I grant, for in my time East India opium has been three guineas a pound, and Turkey eight. And, thirdly, that if you eat a good deal of it, most probably you must... do what is particularly disagreeable to any man of regular habits, viz. die.* These weighty propositions are, all and singular, true. I cannot gainsay them, and truth ever was and will be commendable. But in these three theorems I believe we have exhausted the stock of knowledge as yet accumulated by man on the subject of opium. And therefore, worthy doctors, as there seems to be room for further discoveries, stand aside and allow me to come forward and lecture on this matter.

First, then, it is not so much affirmed as taken for granted, by all who ever mention opium, formally or incidentally, that it does or can produce intoxication. Now, reader, assure yourself, *meo periculo*,* that no quantity of opium ever did or could intoxicate. As to the tincture of opium (commonly called laudanum), *that* might certainly intoxicate if a man could bear to take enough of it. But why? Because it contains so much proof spirit, and not because it contains so much opium. But crude opium, I affirm peremptorily, is incapable of producing any state of body at all resembling that which is produced by alcohol – and not in *degree* only incapable, but even in *kind*: it is not in the quantity of its effects merely, but in the quality that it differs altogether. The pleasure given by wine is always mounting and tending to a crisis, after which it declines. That from opium, when once generated, is stationary for eight or ten hours. The first, to borrow a technical distinction from medicine, is a case of acute – the second, of chronic pleasure: the one is a flame, the other a steady and equable glow. But the main distinction lies in this: that whereas wine disorders the mental faculties, opium, on the contrary (if taken in a proper manner), introduces amongst them the most exquisite order, legislation and harmony. Wine robs a man of his self-possession – opium greatly invigorates it. Wine unsettles and clouds the judgement, and gives a preternatural brightness and a vivid exaltation to the contempts and the admirations, the loves and the hatreds, of the drinker – opium, on the contrary, communicates serenity and equipoise to all the faculties, active or passive, and with respect to the temper and moral feelings in general, it gives simply that sort of vital warmth which is approved by the judgement, and which would probably always accompany a bodily constitution of primeval or antediluvian health. Thus, for instance, opium, like wine, gives an expansion to the heart and the benevolent affections, but then with this remarkable difference: that in the sudden development of kind-heartedness which accompanies inebriation, there is always more or less of a maudlin character, which exposes it to the contempt of the bystander. Men shake hands, swear eternal friendship and shed tears – no mortal knows why, and the sensual creature is clearly uppermost. But the expansion of the benigner feelings incident to opium is no febrile access, but a healthy restoration to that state which the mind would naturally recover upon the removal of any deep-seated irritation of pain that had disturbed and quarrelled with the impulses of a heart originally just and good. True it is that even wine, up to a certain point, and with certain men, rather tends to exalt and to steady the intellect. I myself, who have never been a great wine drinker, used to find that half a dozen glasses of wine advantageously affected the faculties, brightened and intensified the consciousness and gave to the mind a feeling of being "*ponderibus librata suis*".* And certainly it is most absurdly said, in popular language, of any man, that he is *disguised* in liquor. For, on the contrary, most men are disguised by sobriety, and it is when they are drinking (as some old gentleman says in Athenaeus) that men ἑαυτοὺς ἐμφανίζουσιν οἵτινες εἰσίν* – display themselves in their true complexion of character, which surely is not disguising themselves. But still, wine constantly leads a man to the brink of absurdity and extravagance, and, beyond a certain point, it is sure to volatilize and to disperse the intellectual energies, whereas opium always seems to compose what had been agitated and to concentrate what had been distracted. In short, to sum up all in one word, a man who is inebriated, or tending to inebriation, is and feels that he is in a condition which calls up into supremacy the merely human, too often the brutal, part of his nature, but the opium-eater (I speak of him who is not suffering from any disease or other remote effects of opium) feels that the diviner part of his nature is paramount – that is, the moral affections are in a state of cloudless serenity, and over all is the great light of the majestic intellect.*

This is the doctrine of the true Church on the subject of opium – of which Church I acknowledge myself to be the only member, the alpha and the omega, but then it is to be recollected that I speak from the ground of a large and profound personal experience, whereas most of the unscientific* authors who have at all treated of opium, and even of those who have written expressly on the materia medica,* make it evident, from the horror they express of it, that their experimental knowledge of its action is none at all. I will, however, candidly acknowledge that I have met with one person* who bore evidence to its intoxicating power such as staggered my own incredulity, for he was a surgeon and had himself taken opium largely. I happened to say to him that his enemies (as I had heard) charged him with talking nonsense on politics, and that his friends apologized for him by suggesting that he was constantly in a state of intoxication from opium. Now, the accusation, said I, is not prima facie and, of necessity, an absurd one, but the defence *is*. To my surprise, however, he insisted that both his enemies and his friends were in the right: "I will maintain," said he, "that I *do* talk nonsense – and, secondly, I will maintain that I do not talk nonsense upon principle, or with any view to profit, but solely and simply," said he, "solely and simply, solely and simply (repeating it three times over) because I am drunk with opium, and *that* daily." I replied that, as to the allegation of his enemies, as it seemed to be established upon such respectable testimony, seeing that the three parties concerned all agreed in it, it did not become me to question it, but the defence set up I must demur to. He proceeded to discuss the matter and to lay down his reasons, but it seemed to me so impolite to pursue an argument which must have presumed a man mistaken in a point belonging to his own profession that I did not press him even when his course of argument seemed open to objection – not to mention that a man who talks nonsense, even though "with no view to profit", is not altogether the most agreeable partner in a dispute, whether as opponent or respondent. I confess, however, that the authority of a surgeon, and one who was reputed a good one, may seem a weighty one to my prejudice, but still I must plead my experience, which was greater than his greatest by 7,000 drops a day. And, though it was not possible to suppose a medical man unacquainted with the characteristic symptoms of vinous intoxication, it yet struck me that he might proceed on a logical error of using the word intoxication with too great latitude and extending it generically to all modes of nervous excitement, instead of restricting it as the expression for a specific sort of excitement connected with certain diagnostics. Some people have maintained, in my hearing, that they had been drunk upon green tea, and a medical student in London, for whose knowledge in his profession I have reason to feel great respect, assured me the other day that a patient, in recovering from an illness, had got drunk on a beefsteak.

Having dwelt so much on this first and leading error in respect to opium, I shall notice very briefly a second and a third, which are that the elevation of spirits produced by opium is necessarily followed by a proportionate depression, and that the natural and even immediate consequence of opium is torpor and stagnation, animal and mental. The first of these errors I shall content myself with simply denying, assuring my reader that for ten years, during which I took opium at intervals, the day succeeding to that on which I allowed myself this luxury was always a day of unusually good spirits.

With respect to the torpor supposed to follow – or rather (if we were to credit the numerous pictures of Turkish opium-eaters) to accompany the practice of opium-eating – I deny that also. Certainly opium is classed under the head of narcotics, and some such effect it may produce in the end, but the primary effects of opium are always, and in the highest degree, to excite and stimulate the system. This first stage of its action always lasted with me, during my novitiate, for upwards of eight hours, so that it must be the fault of the opium-eater himself if he does not so time his exhibition of the dose (to speak medically) as that the whole weight of its narcotic influence may descend upon his sleep. Turkish opium-eaters, it seems, are absurd enough to sit, like so many equestrian statues, on logs of wood as stupid as themselves. But that the reader may judge of the degree in which opium is likely to stupefy the faculties of an Englishman, I shall (by way of treating the question illustratively, rather than argumentatively) describe the way in which I myself often passed an opium evening in London during the period between 1804 and 1812. It will be seen that at least opium did not move me to seek solitude, and much less to seek inactivity or the torpid state of self-involution ascribed to the Turks. I give this account at the risk of being pronounced a crazy enthusiast or visionary, but I regard *that* little. I must desire my reader to bear in mind that I was a hard student and at severe studies for all the rest of my time, and certainly I had a right occasionally to relaxations as well as other people. These, however, I allowed myself but seldom.

The late Duke of ——* used to say, "Next Friday, by the blessing of Heaven, I purpose to be drunk" – and in like manner I used to fix beforehand how often within a given time and when I would commit a debauch of opium. This was seldom more than once in three weeks, for at that time I could not have ventured to call every day (as I did afterwards) for "a glass of laudanum negus,* warm and without sugar". No, as I have said, I seldom drank laudanum, at that time, more than once in three weeks. This was usually on a Tuesday or a Saturday night – my reason for which was this. In those days Grassini sang at the Opera,* and her voice was delightful to me beyond all that I had ever heard. I know not what may be the state of the Opera House now, having never been within its walls for seven or eight years, but at that time it was by much the most pleasant place of public resort in London for passing an evening. Five shillings admitted one to the gallery, which was subject to far less annoyance than the pit of the theatres; the orchestra was distinguished by its sweet and melodious grandeur from all English orchestras – the composition of which, I confess, is not acceptable to my ear, from the predominance of the clangorous instruments and the absolute tyranny of the violin. The choruses were divine to hear, and when Grassini appeared in some interlude, as she often did, and poured forth her passionate soul as Andromache at the tomb of Hector* etc., I question whether any Turk, of all that ever entered the paradise of opium-eaters, can have had half the pleasure I had. But, indeed, I honour the barbarians too much by supposing them capable of any pleasures approaching to the intellectual ones of an Englishman. For music is an intellectual or a sensual pleasure, according to the temperament of him who hears it. And, by the by, with the exception of the fine extravaganza on that subject in *Twelfth Night*,* I do not recollect more than one thing said adequately on the subject of music in all literature: it is a passage in the *Religio Medici* of Sir T. Browne* – and, though chiefly remarkable for its sublimity, has also a philosophic value, inasmuch as it points to the true theory of musical effects. The mistake of most people is to suppose that it is by the ear they communicate with music, and, therefore, that they are purely passive to its effects. But this is not so: it is by the reaction of the mind upon the notices of the ear (the *matter* coming by the senses, the *form* from the mind) that the pleasure is constructed, and therefore it is that people of equally good ear differ so much in this point from one another. Now opium, by greatly increasing the activity of the mind generally, increases of necessity that particular mode of its activity by which we are able to construct out of the raw material of organic sound an elaborate intellectual pleasure. But, says a friend, a succession of musical sounds is to me like a collection of Arabic characters: I can attach no ideas to them. Ideas, my good sir? There is no occasion for them. All that class of ideas which can be available in such a case has a language of representative feelings. But this is a subject foreign to my present purposes. It is sufficient to say that a chorus etc. of elaborate harmony displayed before me as in a piece of arras work the whole of my past life, not as if recalled by an act of memory, but as if present and incarnated in the music – no longer painful to dwell upon, but the detail of its incidents removed, or blended in some hazy abstraction, and its passions exalted, spiritualized and sublimed. All this was to be had for five shillings. And over and above the music of the stage and the orchestra, I had all around me, in the intervals of the performance, the music of the Italian language talked by Italian women, for the gallery was usually crowded with Italians, and I listened with a pleasure such as that with which Weld the traveller lay and listened, in Canada, to the sweet laughter of Indian women* – for the less you understand of a language, the more sensible you are to the melody or harshness of its sounds. For such a purpose, therefore, it was an advantage to me that I was a poor Italian scholar, reading it but little and not speaking it at all, nor understanding a tenth part of what I heard spoken.

These were my opera pleasures, but another pleasure I had which, as it could be had only on a Saturday night, occasionally struggled with my love of the opera, for at that time Tuesday and Saturday were the regular opera nights. On this subject I am afraid I shall be rather obscure, but, I can assure the reader, not at all more so than Marinus in his life of Proclus* or many other biographers and autobiographers of fair reputation. This pleasure, I have said, was to be had only on a Saturday night. What then was Saturday night to me more than any other night? I had no labours that I rested from – no wages to receive: what needed I to care for Saturday night more than as it was a summons to hear Grassini? True, most logical reader, what you say is unanswerable. And yet so it was and is that whereas different men throw their feelings into different channels, and most are apt to show their interest in the concerns of the poor chiefly by sympathy expressed in some shape or other with their distresses and sorrows, I at that time was disposed to express my interest by sympathizing with their pleasures. The pains of poverty I had lately seen too much of – more than I wished to remember – but the pleasures of the poor, their consolations of spirit and their reposes from bodily toil can never become oppressive to contemplate. Now, Saturday night is the season for the chief, regular and periodic return of rest to the poor. In this point the most hostile sects unite and acknowledge a common link of brotherhood: almost all Christendom rests from its labours. It is a rest introductory to another rest, and divided by a whole day and two nights from the renewal of toil. On this account I feel always, on a Saturday night, as though I also were released from some yoke of labour, had some wages to receive and some luxury of repose to enjoy. For the sake, therefore, of witnessing, upon as large a scale as possible, a spectacle with which my sympathy was so entire, I used often, on Saturday nights, after I had taken opium, to wander forth, without much regarding the direction or the distance, to all the markets and other parts of London to which the poor resort on a Saturday night for laying out their wages. Many a family party, consisting of a man, his wife and sometimes one or two of his children, have I listened to as they stood consulting on their ways and means, or the strength of their exchequer, or the price of household articles. Gradually I became familiar with their wishes, their difficulties and their opinions. Sometimes there might be heard murmurs of discontent, but far oftener expressions on the countenance, or uttered in words, of patience, hope and tranquillity. And taken generally, I must say that, in this point at least, the poor are far more philosophic than the rich – that they show a more ready and cheerful submission to what they consider as irremediable evils or irreparable losses. Whenever I saw occasion or could do it without appearing to be intrusive, I joined their parties and gave my opinion upon the matter in discussion – which, if not always judicious, was always received indulgently. If wages were a little higher, or expected to be so, or the quartern loaf* a little lower, or it was reported that onions and butter were expected to fall, I was glad, yet if the contrary were true, I drew from opium some means of consoling myself. For opium (like the bee that extracts its materials indiscriminately from roses and from the soot of chimneys)* can overrule all feelings into a compliance with the master key. Some of these rambles led me to great distances, for an opium-eater is too happy to observe the motion of time. And sometimes, in my attempts to steer homewards, upon nautical principles by fixing my eye on the Pole Star and seeking ambitiously for a Northwest Passage instead of circumnavigating all the capes and headlands, I had doubled in my outward voyage, I came suddenly upon such knotty problems of alleys, such enigmatical entries and such Sphinx's riddles of streets without thoroughfares as must, I conceive, baffle the audacity of porters and confound the intellects of hackney coachmen. I could almost have believed, at times, that I must be the first discoverer of some of these *terræ incognitæ*,* and doubted whether they had yet been laid down in the modern charts of London. For all this, however, I paid a heavy price in distant years, when the human face tyrannized over my dreams, and the perplexities of my steps in London came back and haunted my sleep with the feeling of perplexities moral or intellectual that brought confusion to the reason or anguish and remorse to the conscience.

Thus I have shown that opium does not, of necessity, produce inactivity or torpor, but that on the contrary it often led me into markets and theatres. Yet, in candour, I will admit that markets and theatres are not the appropriate haunts of the opium-eater when in the divinest state incident to his enjoyment. In that state, crowds become an oppression to him – music, even, too sensual and gross. He naturally seeks solitude and silence as indispensable conditions of those trances, or profoundest reveries, which are the crown and consummation of what opium can do for human nature. I, whose disease it was to meditate too much and to observe too little, and who, upon my first entrance at college, was nearly falling into a deep melancholy from brooding too much on the sufferings which I had witnessed in London, was sufficiently aware of the tendencies of my own thoughts to do all I could to counteract them. I was, indeed, like a person who, according to the old legend, had entered the cave of Trophonius,* and the remedies I sought were to force myself into society and to keep my understanding in continual activity upon matters of science. But for these remedies, I should certainly have become hypochondriacally melancholy. In after years, however, when my cheerfulness was more fully re-established, I yielded to my natural inclination for a solitary life. And, at that time, I often fell into these reveries upon taking opium, and more than once it has happened to me on a summer night, when I have been at an open window, in a room from which I could overlook the sea at a mile below me and could command a view of the great town of L——* at about the same distance, that I have sat, from sunset to sunrise, motionless and without wishing to move.

I shall be charged with mysticism, Behmenism, quietism,* etc., but *that* shall not alarm me. Sir H. Vane the Younger* was one of our wisest men, and let my readers see if he, in his philosophical works, be half as unmystical as I am. I say, then, that it has often struck me that the scene itself was somewhat typical of what took place in such a reverie. The town of L—— represented the earth, with its sorrows and its graves left behind, yet not out of sight, nor wholly forgotten. The ocean, in everlasting but gentle agitation, and brooded over by a dove-like calm, might not unfitly typify the mind and the mood which then swayed it. For it seemed to me as if then first I stood at a distance and aloof from the uproar of life – as if the tumult, the fever and the strife were suspended, a respite granted from the secret burdens of the heart, a sabbath of repose, a resting from human labours. Here were the hopes which blossom in the paths of life reconciled with the peace which is in the grave – motions of the intellect as unwearied as the heavens, yet for all anxieties a halcyon calm: a tranquillity that seemed no product of inertia, but as if resulting from mighty and equal antagonisms, infinite activities, infinite repose.

O just, subtle and mighty opium,* that to the hearts of poor and rich alike, for the wounds that will never heal and for "the pangs that tempt the spirit to rebel",* bringest an assuaging balm! Eloquent opium, that with thy potent rhetoric stealest away the purposes of wrath, and to the guilty man for one night givest back the hopes of his youth, and hands washed pure from blood, and to the proud man a brief oblivion for

> Wrongs unredress'd and insults unavenged,*

that summonest to the Chancery of dreams, for the triumphs of suffering innocence, false witnesses, and confoundest perjury, and dost reverse the sentences of unrighteous judges – thou buildest upon the bosom of darkness, out of the fantastic imagery of the brain, cities and temples beyond the art of Phidias and Praxiteles,* beyond the splendour of Babylon and Hekatómpylos,* and "from the anarchy of dreaming sleep"* callest into sunny light the faces of long-buried beauties and the blessed household countenances cleansed from the "dishonours of the grave"!* Thou only givest these gifts to man, and thou hast the keys of paradise, O just, subtle and mighty opium!

INTRODUCTION TO THE PAINS OF OPIUM

COURTEOUS AND, I HOPE, indulgent reader (for all *my* readers must be indulgent ones, or else, I fear, I shall shock them too much to count on their courtesy), having accompanied me thus far, now let me request you to move onwards for about eight years – that is to say, from 1804 (when I have said that my acquaintance with opium first began) to 1812. The years of academic life are now over and gone, almost forgotten – the student's cap no longer presses my temples. If my cap exist at all, it presses those of some youthful scholar, I trust, as happy as myself, and as passionate a lover of knowledge. My gown is, by this time, I dare to say, in the same condition with many thousands of excellent books in the Bodleian – viz., diligently perused by certain studious moths and worms, or departed, however (which is all that I know of its fate), to that great reservoir of *somewhere* to which all the teacups, tea caddies, teapots, tea kettles, etc., have departed (not to speak of still frailer vessels, such as glasses, decanters, bed-makers,* etc.) which occasional resemblances in the present generation of tea-cups etc. remind me of having once possessed, but of whose departure and final fate I, in common with most gownsmen of either university, could give, I suspect, but an obscure and conjectural history. The persecutions of the chapel bell, sounding its unwelcome summons to six o'clock matins, interrupts my slumbers no longer: the porter who rang it, upon whose beautiful nose (bronze, inlaid with copper) I wrote, in retaliation, so many Greek epigrams whilst I was dressing, is dead, and has ceased to disturb anybody – and I and many others who suffered much from his tintinnabulous* propensities have now agreed to overlook his errors and have forgiven him. Even with the bell I am now in charity: it rings, I suppose, as formerly, thrice a day, and cruelly annoys, I doubt not, many worthy gentlemen, and disturbs their peace of mind, but as to me, in this year 1812, I regard its treacherous voice no longer ("treacherous" I call it, for, by some refinement of malice, it spoke in as sweet and silvery tones as if it had been inviting one to a party). Its tones have no longer, indeed, power to reach me, let the wind sit as favourable as the malice of the bell itself could wish, for I am 250 miles away from it, and buried in the depth of mountains. And what am I doing amongst the mountains? Taking opium. Yes, but what else? Why, reader, in 1812, the year we are now arrived at, as well as for some years previous, I have been chiefly studying German metaphysics in the writings of Kant, Fichte, Schelling, etc.* And how, and in what manner, do I live? In short, what class or description of men do I belong to? I am at this period, viz. in 1812, living in a cottage, and with a single female servant (*honi soit qui mal y pense*),* who, amongst my neighbours, passes by the name of my "housekeeper".* And, as a scholar and a man of learned education, and in that sense a gentleman, I may presume to class myself as an unworthy member of that indefinite body called "gentlemen". Partly on the ground I have assigned, perhaps – partly because, from my having no visible calling or business, it is rightly judged that I must be living on my private fortune* – I am so classed by my neighbours. And, by the courtesy of modern England, I am usually addressed on letters etc. "Esquire", though having, I fear, in the rigorous construction of heralds, but slender pretensions to that distinguished honour.* Yes, in popular estimation I am X.Y.Z., Esquire, but not Justice of the Peace, nor Custos Rotulorum.* Am I married? Not yet. And I still take opium? On Saturday nights. And, perhaps, have taken it unblushingly ever since "the rainy Sunday" and "the stately Pantheon" and "the beatific druggist" of 1804? Even so. And how do I find my health after all this opium-eating? In short, how do I do? Why, pretty well, I thank you, reader: in the phrase of ladies in the straw,* "as well as can be expected". In fact, if I dared to say the real and simple truth, though to satisfy the theories of medical men I *ought* to be ill, I never was better in my life than in the spring of 1812, and I hope sincerely that the quantity of claret, port or "particular Madeira"* which in all probability you, good reader, have taken and design to take for every term of eight years during your natural life may as little disorder your health as mine was disordered by the opium I had taken for the eight years between 1804 and 1812. Hence you may see again the danger of taking any medical advice from *Anastasius*. In divinity, for aught I know, or law, he may be a safe counsellor, but not in medicine. No: it is far better to consult Dr Buchan,* as I did, for I never forgot that worthy man's excellent suggestion, and I was "particularly careful not to take above five-and-twenty ounces of laudanum". To this moderation and temperate use of the article I may ascribe it, I suppose, that as yet, at least (i.e. in 1812), I am ignorant and unsuspicious of the avenging terrors which opium has in store for those who abuse its lenity. At the same time, it must not be forgotten that hitherto I have been only a dilettante eater of opium: eight years' practice even, with the single precaution of allowing sufficient intervals between every indulgence, has not been sufficient to make opium necessary to me as an article of daily diet. But now comes a different era. Move on, if you please, reader, to 1813. In the summer of the year we have just quitted, I had suffered much in bodily health from distress of mind connected with a very melancholy event.* This event, being no ways related to the subject now before me further than through the bodily illness which it produced, I need not more particularly notice. Whether this illness of 1812 had any share in that of 1813, I know not, but so it was that in the latter year I was attacked by a most appalling irritation of the stomach, in all respects the same as that which had caused me so much suffering in youth, and accompanied by a revival of all the old dreams. This is the point of my narrative on which, as respects my own self-justification, the whole of what follows may be said to hinge. And here I find myself in a perplexing dilemma.

Either, on the one hand, I must exhaust the reader's patience by such a detail of my malady and of my struggles with it as might suffice to establish the fact of my inability to wrestle any longer with irritation and constant suffering, or on the other hand, by passing lightly over this critical part of my story, I must forgo the benefit of a stronger impression left on the mind of the reader and must lay myself open to the misconstruction of having slipped, by the easy and gradual steps of self-indulging persons, from the first to the final stage of opium-eating (a misconstruction to which there will be a lurking predisposition in most readers, from my previous acknowledgements). This is the dilemma, the first horn of which would be sufficient to toss and gore any column of patient readers, though drawn up sixteen deep and constantly relieved by fresh men. Consequently, *that* is not to be thought of. It remains then that I *postulate* so much as is necessary for my purpose. And let me take as full credit for what I postulate as if I had demonstrated it, good reader, at the expense of your patience and my own. Be not so ungenerous as to let me suffer in your good opinion through my own forbearance and regard for your comfort. No: believe all that I ask of you, viz. that I could resist no longer – believe it liberally, and as an act of grace, or else in mere prudence, for, if not, then in the next edition of my 'Opium Confessions', revised and enlarged, I will make you believe and tremble, and *à force d'ennuyer,** by mere dint of pandiculation,* I will terrify all readers of mine from ever again questioning any postulate that I shall think fit to make.

This then, let me repeat: I postulate that at the time I began to take opium daily I could not have done otherwise. Whether, indeed, afterwards I might not have succeeded in breaking off the habit, even when it seemed to me that all efforts would be unavailing – and whether many of the innumerable efforts which I *did* make might not have been carried much further and my gradual reconquests of ground lost might not have been followed up much more energetically – these are questions which I must decline. Perhaps I might make out a case of palliation, but shall I speak ingenuously? I confess it, as a besetting infirmity of mine, that I am too much of a eudemonist.* I hanker too much after a state of happiness, both for myself and others. I cannot face misery, whether my own or not, with an eye of sufficient firmness, and am little capable of encountering present pain for the sake of any reversionary benefit. On some other matters, I can agree with the gentlemen in the cotton trade* at Manchester in affecting the Stoic philosophy, but not in this. Here I take the liberty of an Eclectic* philosopher, and I look out for some courteous and considerate sect that will condescend more to the infirm condition of an opium-eater – that are "sweet men", as Chaucer says, "to give absolution",* and will show some conscience in the penances they inflict and the efforts of abstinence they exact from poor sinners like myself. An inhuman moralist I can no more endure in my nervous state than opium that has not been boiled. At any rate, he who summons me to send out a large freight of self-denial and mortification upon any cruising voyage of moral improvement must make it clear to my understanding that the concern is a hopeful one. At my time of life (six-and-thirty years of age), it cannot be supposed that I have much energy to spare. In fact, I find it all little enough for the intellectual labours I have on my hands, and therefore let no man expect to frighten me by a few hard words into embarking any part of it upon desperate adventures of morality.

Whether desperate or not, however, the issue of the struggle in 1813 was what I have mentioned, and from this date the reader is to consider me as a regular and confirmed opium-eater, of whom to ask whether on any particular day he had or had not taken opium would be to ask whether his lungs had performed respiration or the heart fulfilled its functions. You understand now, reader, what I am, and you are by this time aware that no old gentleman "with a snow-white beard" will have any chance of persuading me to surrender "the little golden receptacle of the pernicious drug".* No: I give notice to all, whether moralists or surgeons, that whatever be their pretensions and skill in their respective lines of practice, they must not hope for any countenance from me if they think to begin by any savage proposition for a Lent or Ramadan of abstinence from opium. This then being all fully understood between us, we shall in future sail before the wind. Now then, reader, from 1813, where all this time we have been sitting down and loitering, rise up, if you please, and walk forward about three years more. Now draw up the curtain, and you shall see me in a new character.

If any man, poor or rich, were to say that he would tell us what had been the happiest day in his life, and the why and the wherefore, I suppose that we should all cry out, "Hear him! Hear him!" As to the happiest *day*, that must be very difficult for any wise man to name, because any event that could occupy so distinguished a place in a man's retrospect of his life, or be entitled to have shed a special felicity on any one day, ought to be of such an enduring character as that (accidents apart) it should have continued to shed the same felicity, or one not distinguishably less, on many years together. To the happiest *lustrum*,* however, or even to the happiest *year*, it may be allowed to any man to point without discountenance from wisdom. This year, in my case, reader, was the one which we have now reached, though it stood,

I confess, as a parenthesis between years of a gloomier character. It was a year of brilliant water (to speak after the manner of jewellers), set, as it were, and insulated – in the gloom and cloudy melancholy of opium. Strange as it may sound, I had a little before this time descended suddenly, and without any considerable effort, from 320 grains of opium (i.e. eight thousand drops* of laudanum) per day to forty grains, or one-eighth part. Instantaneously, and as if by magic, the cloud of profoundest melancholy which rested upon my brain like some black vapours that I have seen roll away from the summits of mountains drew off in one day (νυχθήμερον)* – passed off with its murky banners as simultaneously as a ship that has been stranded and is floated off by a spring tide

That moveth altogether, if it move at all.*

Now, then, I was again happy. I now took only 1,000 drops of laudanum per day, and what was that? A latter spring had come to close up the season of youth: my brain performed its functions as healthily as ever before; I read Kant again, and again I understood him, or fancied that I did. Again my feelings of pleasure expanded themselves to all around me, and if any man from Oxford or Cambridge, or from neither, had been announced to me in my unpretending cottage, I should have welcomed him with as sumptuous a reception as so poor a man could offer. Whatever else was wanting to a wise man's happiness, of laudanum I would have given him as much as he wished, and in a golden cup. And, by the way, now that I speak of giving laudanum away, I remember, about this time, a little incident – which I mention because, trifling as it was, the reader will soon meet it again in my dreams, which it influenced more fearfully than could be imagined. One day a Malay knocked at my door. What business a Malay could have to transact amongst English mountains I cannot conjecture, but possibly he was on his road to a seaport about forty miles distant.

The servant who opened the door to him was a young girl born and bred amongst the mountains,* who had never seen an Asiatic dress of any sort. His turban, therefore, confounded her not a little, and as it turned out that his attainments in English were exactly of the same extent as hers in the Malay, there seemed to be an impassable gulf fixed between all communication of ideas, if either party had happened to possess any. In this dilemma, the girl, recollecting the reputed learning of her master (and, doubtless, giving me credit for a knowledge of all the languages of the earth – besides, perhaps, a few of the lunar ones), came and gave me to understand that there was a sort of demon below, whom she clearly imagined that my art could exorcise from the house. I did not immediately go down, but, when I did, the group which presented itself, arranged as it was by accident, though not very elaborate, took hold of my fancy and my eye in a way that none of the statuesque attitudes exhibited in the ballets at the Opera House, though so ostentatiously complex, had ever done. In a cottage kitchen but panelled on the wall with dark wood that from age and rubbing resembled oak, and looking more like a rustic hall of entrance than a kitchen, stood the Malay, his turban and loose trousers of dingy white relieved upon the dark panelling. He had placed himself nearer to the girl than she seemed to relish, though her native spirit of mountain intrepidity contended with the feeling of simple awe which her countenance expressed as she gazed upon the tiger-cat before her. And a more striking picture there could not be imagined than the beautiful English face of the girl and its exquisite fairness, together with her erect and independent attitude, contrasted with the sallow and bilious skin of the Malay, enamelled or veneered with mahogany by marine air, his small, fierce, restless eyes, thin lips, slavish gestures and adorations. Half-hidden by the ferocious-looking Malay was a little child from a neighbouring cottage who had crept in after him and was now in the act of reverting its head and gazing upwards at the turban and the fiery eyes beneath it, whilst with one hand he caught at the dress of the young woman for protection. My knowledge of the oriental tongues is not remarkably extensive, being indeed confined to two words: the Arabic word for "barley", and the Turkish for "opium" (*madjoon*), which I have learnt from *Anastasius*. And as I had neither a Malay dictionary nor even Adelung's *Mithridates*,* which might have helped me to a few words, I addressed him in some lines from the *Iliad*, considering that, of such languages as I possessed, Greek, in point of longitude, came geographically nearest to an oriental one. He worshipped me in a most devout manner, and replied in what I suppose was Malay. In this way I saved my reputation with my neighbours, for the Malay had no means of betraying the secret. He lay down upon the floor for about an hour, and then pursued his journey. On his departure, I presented him with a piece of opium. To him, as an orientalist, I concluded that opium must be familiar, and the expression of his face convinced me that it was. Nevertheless, I was struck with some little consternation when I saw him suddenly raise his hand to his mouth and (in the schoolboy phrase) bolt the whole, divided into three pieces, at one mouthful. The quantity was enough to kill three dragoons and their horses, and I felt some alarm for the poor creature, but what could be done? I had given him the opium in compassion for his solitary life, on recollecting that if he had travelled on foot from London it must be nearly three weeks since he could have exchanged a thought with any human being. I could not think of violating the laws of hospitality by having him seized and drenched with an emetic, and thus frightening him into a notion that we were going to sacrifice him to some English idol. No, there was clearly no help for it. He took his leave, and for some days I felt anxious, but as I never heard of any Malay being found dead, I became convinced that he was used to opium* and that I must have done him the service I designed by giving him one night of respite from the pains of wandering.

This incident I have digressed to mention because this Malay (partly from the picturesque exhibition he assisted to frame, partly from the anxiety I connected with his image for some days) fastened afterwards upon my dreams and brought other Malays with him worse than himself, that ran "a-muck"* at me and led me into a world of troubles. But to quit this episode and to return to my intercalary* year of happiness. I have said already that on a subject so important to us all as happiness, we should listen with pleasure to any man's experience or experiments, even though he were but a ploughboy who cannot be supposed to have ploughed very deep into such an intractable soil as that of human pains and pleasures, or to have conducted his researches upon any very enlightened principles. But I, who have taken happiness both in a solid and a liquid shape, both boiled and unboiled, both East India and Turkey, who have conducted my experiments upon this interesting subject with a sort of galvanic battery and have, for the general benefit of the world, inoculated myself, as it were, with the poison of 8,000 drops of laudanum per day (just, for the same reason, as a French surgeon inoculated himself lately with cancer, an English one twenty years ago with plague and a third, I know not of what nation, with hydrophobia),* *I* (it will be admitted) must surely know what happiness is, if anybody does. And therefore I will here lay down an analysis of happiness, and as the most interesting mode of communicating it I will give it not didactically, but wrapped up and involved in a picture of one evening, as I spent every evening during the intercalary year when laudanum, though taken daily, was to me no more than the elixir of pleasure. This done, I shall quit the subject of happiness altogether and pass to a very different one – the *pains of opium*.

Let there be a cottage, standing in a valley, eighteen miles from any town: no spacious valley, but about two miles long by three quarters of a mile in average width – the benefit of which provision is that all the families resident within its circuit will compose, as it were, one larger household personally familiar to your eye and more or less interesting to your affections. Let the mountains be real mountains, between three and four thousand feet high, and the cottage a real cottage, not (as a witty author has it) "a cottage with a double coach-house".* Let it be, in fact (for I must abide by the actual scene), a white cottage embowered with flowering shrubs so chosen as to unfold a succession of flowers upon the walls and clustering round the windows through all the months of spring, summer and autumn – beginning, in fact, with May roses and ending with jasmine. Let it, however, *not* be spring, nor summer, nor autumn, but winter, in his sternest shape. This is a most important point in the science of happiness. And I am surprised to see people overlook it and think it matter of congratulation that winter is going – or, if coming, is not likely to be a severe one. On the contrary, I put up a petition annually for as much snow, hail, frost or storm, of one kind or other, as the skies can possibly afford us. Surely everybody is aware of the divine pleasures which attend a winter fireside, candles at four o'clock, warm hearthrugs, tea, a fair tea-maker, shutters closed, curtains flowing in ample draperies on the floor, whilst the wind and rain are raging audibly without,

> And at the doors and windows seem to call,
> As heav'n and earth they would together mell;
> Yet the least entrance find they none at all,
> Whence sweeter grows our rest secure in massy hall.
>
> *Castle of Indolence**

All these are items in the description of a winter evening which must surely be familiar to everybody born in a high latitude. And it is evident that most of these delicacies, like ice cream, require a very low temperature of the atmosphere to produce them: they are fruits which cannot be ripened without weather stormy or inclement, in some way or other. I am not "particular", as people say, whether it be snow or black frost, or wind so strong that (as Mr —— says) "you may lean your back against it like a post".* I can put up even with rain, provided it rains cats and dogs, but something of the sort I must have. And if I have it not, I think myself in a manner ill-used, for why am I called on to pay so heavily for winter in coals and candles and various privations that will occur even to gentlemen, if I am not to have the article good of its kind? No: a Canadian winter for my money, or a Russian one, where every man is but a co-proprietor with the north wind in the fee-simple* of his own ears. Indeed, so great an epicure am I in this matter that I cannot relish a winter night fully if it be much past St Thomas's Day* and have degenerated into disgusting tendencies to vernal appearances. No, it must be divided by a thick wall of dark nights from all return of light and sunshine. From the latter weeks of October to Christmas Eve, therefore, is the period during which happiness is in season – which, in my judgement, enters the room with the tea tray, for tea, though ridiculed by those who are naturally of coarse nerves or are become so from wine-drinking and are not susceptible of influence from so refined a stimulant, will always be the favourite beverage of the intellectual. And, for my part, I would have joined Dr Johnson in a *bellum internecinum* against Jonas Hanway,* or any other impious person who should presume to disparage it. But here, to save myself the trouble of too much verbal description, I will introduce a painter and give him directions for the rest of the picture. Painters do not like white cottages, unless a good deal weather-stained, but as the reader now understands that it is a winter night, his services will not be required, except for the inside of the house.

Paint me, then, a room seventeen feet by twelve, and not more than seven and a half feet high. This, reader, is somewhat ambitiously styled, in my family, the "drawing room", but, being contrived "a double debt to pay",* it is also and more justly termed the library, for it happens that books are the only article of property in which I am richer than my neighbours. Of these, I have about five thousand, collected gradually since my eighteenth year. Therefore, painter, put as many as you can into this room. Make it populous with books, and, furthermore, paint me a good fire and furniture plain and modest, befitting the unpretending cottage of a scholar. And, near the fire, paint me a tea table, and (as it is clear that no creature can come to see one such a stormy night) place only two cups and saucers on the tea tray – and, if you know how to paint such a thing symbolically or otherwise, paint me an eternal teapot (eternal *a parte ante* and *a parte post*,* for I usually drink tea from eight o'clock at night to four o'clock in the morning). And, as it is very unpleasant to make tea, or to pour it out for oneself, paint me a lovely young woman sitting at the table. Paint her arms like Aurora's, and her smiles like Hebe's*... But no, dear M., not even in jest let me insinuate that thy power to illuminate my cottage rests upon a tenure so perishable as mere personal beauty, or that the witchcraft of angelic smiles lies within the empire of any earthly pencil. Pass, then, my good painter, to something more within its power, and the next article brought forward should naturally be myself – a picture of the Opium-Eater, with his "little golden receptacle of the pernicious drug" lying beside him on the table. As to the opium, I have no objection to see a picture of *that*, though I would rather see the original. You may paint it if you choose, but I apprize you that no "little" receptacle would, even in 1816, answer *my* purpose, who was at a distance from the "stately Pantheon" and all druggists (mortal or otherwise). No: you may as well paint the real receptacle, which was not of gold, but of glass, and as much like a wine decanter as possible. Into this you may put a quart of ruby-coloured laudanum. That, and a book of German metaphysics placed by its side, will sufficiently attest my being in the neighbourhood, but as to myself, there I demur. I admit that, naturally, I ought to occupy the foreground of the picture – that being the hero of the piece, or (if you choose) the criminal at the bar, my body should be had into court. This seems reasonable, but why should I confess, on this point, to a painter? Or why confess at all? If the public (into whose private ear I am confidentially whispering my confessions, and not into any painter's) should chance to have framed some agreeable picture for itself of the Opium-Eater's exterior, should have ascribed to him, romantically, an elegant person, or a handsome face, why should I barbarously tear from it so pleasing a delusion – pleasing both to the public and to me? No, paint me, if at all, according to your own fancy, and as a painter's fancy should teem with beautiful creations, I cannot fail, in that way, to be a gainer. And now, reader, we have run through all the ten categories of my condition as it stood about 1816–17, up to the middle of which latter year I judge myself to have been a happy man, and the elements of that happiness I have endeavoured to place before you in the above sketch of the interior of a scholar's library in a cottage among the mountains on a stormy winter evening.

But now farewell – a long farewell to happiness, winter or summer! Farewell to smiles and laughter! Farewell to peace of mind! Farewell to hope and to tranquil dreams, and to the blessed consolations of sleep!* For more than three years and a half I am summoned away from these. I am now arrived at an Iliad of woes, for I have now to record

THE PAINS OF OPIUM

> ...as when some great painter dips
> His pencil in the gloom of earthquake and eclipse.
> Shelley's *Revolt of Islam*.*

READER, WHO HAVE THUS FAR accompanied me, I must request your attention to a brief explanatory note on three points:

1. For several reasons, I have not been able to compose the notes for this part of my narrative into any regular and connected shape. I give the notes disjointed as I find them, or have now drawn them up from memory. Some of them point to their own date, some I have dated, and some are

undated. Whenever it could answer my purpose to transplant them from the natural or chronological order, I have not scrupled to do so. Sometimes I speak in the present, sometimes in the past tense. Few of the notes, perhaps, were written exactly at the period of time to which they relate, but this can little affect their accuracy, as the impressions were such that they can never fade from my mind. Much has been omitted. I could not, without effort, constrain myself to the task of either recalling or constructing into a regular narrative the whole burden of horrors which lies upon my brain. This feeling partly I plead in excuse, and partly that I am now in London and am a helpless sort of person who cannot even arrange his own papers without assistance, and I am separated from the hands which are wont to perform for me the offices of an amanuensis.

2. You will think, perhaps, that I am too confidential and communicative of my own private history. It may be so. But my way of writing is rather to think aloud and follow my own humours than much to consider who is listening to me, and if I stop to consider what is proper to be said to this or that person, I shall soon come to doubt whether any part at all is proper. The fact is, I place myself at a distance of fifteen or twenty years ahead of this time, and suppose myself writing to those who will be interested about me hereafter. And wishing to have some record of a time the entire history of which no one can know but myself, I do it as fully as I am able with the efforts I am now capable of making, because I know not whether I can ever find time to do it again.

3. It will occur to you often to ask why did I not release myself from the horrors of opium by leaving it off or diminishing it. To this I must answer briefly: it might be supposed that I yielded to the fascinations of opium too easily; it

cannot be supposed that any man can be charmed by its terrors. The reader may be sure, therefore, that I made attempts innumerable to reduce the quantity. I add that those who witnessed the agonies of those attempts, and not myself, were the first to beg me to desist. But could not I have reduced it a drop a day or, by adding water, have bisected or trisected a drop? A thousand drops bisected would thus have taken nearly six years to reduce, and that way would certainly not have answered. But this is a common mistake of those who know nothing of opium experimentally. I appeal to those who do whether it is not always found that down to a certain point it can be reduced with ease and even pleasure, but that after that point further reduction causes intense suffering. Yes, say many thoughtless persons who know not what they are talking of, you will suffer a little low spirits and dejection for a few days. I answer, no, there is nothing like low spirits. On the contrary, the mere animal spirits are uncommonly raised, the pulse is improved, the health is better. It is not there that the suffering lies. It has no resemblance to the sufferings caused by renouncing wine. It is a state of unutterable irritation of stomach (which surely is not much like dejection), accompanied by intense perspirations and feelings such as I shall not attempt to describe without more space at my command.

I shall now enter "*in medias res*",* and shall anticipate, from a time when my opium pains might be said to be at their acme, an account of their palsying effects on the intellectual faculties.

* * *

My studies have now been long interrupted. I cannot read to myself with any pleasure – hardly with a moment's endurance. Yet, I read aloud sometimes for the pleasure of others, because reading is an accomplishment of mine and, in the slang use of the word *accomplishment* as a superficial and ornamental attainment, almost the only one I possess. And formerly, if I had any vanity at all connected with any endowment or attainment of mine, it was with this, for I had observed that no accomplishment was so rare. Players are the worst readers of all: —— reads vilely, and Mrs ——,* who is so celebrated, can read nothing well but dramatic compositions: Milton she cannot read sufferably. People in general either read poetry without any passion at all, or else overstep the modesty of nature and read not like scholars. Of late, if I have felt moved by anything in books, it has been by the grand lamentations of *Samson Agonistes*, or the great harmonies of the Satanic speeches in *Paradise Regained*,* when read aloud by myself. A young lady sometimes comes and drinks tea with us: at her request and M.'s I now and then read W——'s poems to them.* (W., by the by, is the only poet I ever met who could read his own verses: often indeed he reads admirably.)

For nearly two years I believe that I read no book but one, and I owe it to the author, in discharge of a great debt of gratitude, to mention what that was. The sublimer and more passionate poets I still read, as I have said, by snatches, and occasionally. But my proper vocation, as I well knew, was the exercise of the analytic understanding. Now, for the most part, analytic studies are continuous and not to be pursued by fits and starts or fragmentary efforts. Mathematics, for instance, intellectual philosophy, etc. were all become insupportable to me. I shrunk from them with a sense of powerless and infantine feebleness that gave me an anguish the greater from remembering the time when I grappled with them to my own hourly delight – and for this further reason: because I had devoted the labour of my whole life and had dedicated my intellect, blossoms and fruits to the slow and elaborate toil of constructing one single work, to which I had presumed to give the title of an unfinished work of Spinoza's, viz. *De emendatione humani intellectus.** This was now lying locked up, as by frost, like any Spanish bridge or aqueduct begun upon too great a scale for the resources of the architect. And instead of surviving me as a monument of wishes at least, and aspirations, and a life of labour dedicated to the exaltation of human nature in that way in which God had best fitted me to promote so great an object, it was likely to stand a memorial to my children of hopes defeated, of baffled efforts, of materials uselessly accumulated, of foundations laid that were never to support a superstructure – of the grief and the ruin of the architect. In this state of imbecility, I had, for amusement, turned my attention to political economy. My understanding, which formerly had been as active and restless as a hyena, could not, I suppose (so long as I lived at all) sink into utter lethargy – and political economy offers this advantage to a person in my state: that though it is eminently an organic science (no part, that is to say, but what acts on the whole, as the whole again reacts on each part), yet the several parts may be detached and contemplated singly. Great as was the prostration of my powers at this time, yet I could not forget my knowledge, and my understanding had been for too many years intimate with severe thinkers, with logic and the great masters of knowledge, not to be aware of the utter feebleness of the main herd of modern economists. I had been led in 1811 to look into loads of books and pamphlets on many branches of economy, and, at my desire, M. sometimes read to me chapters from more recent works or parts of parliamentary debates. I saw that these were generally the very dregs and rinsings of the human intellect, and that any man of sound head and practised in wielding logic with a scholastic adroitness might take up the whole academy of modern economists and throttle them between heaven and earth with his finger and thumb, or bray their fungus heads to powder with a lady's fan. At length, in 1819, a friend in Edinburgh sent me down Mr Ricardo's book,* and recurring to my own prophetic anticipation of the advent of some legislator for this science, I said, before I had finished the first chapter, "Thou art the man!"* Wonder and curiosity were emotions that had long been dead in me. Yet I wondered once more: I wondered at myself that I could once again be stimulated to the effort of reading, and much more I wondered at the book. Had this profound work been really written in England during the nineteenth century? Was it possible? I supposed thinking* had been extinct in England. Could it be that an Englishman, and he not in academic bowers, but oppressed by mercantile and senatorial cares,* had accomplished what all the universities of Europe and a century of thought had failed even to advance by one hair's breadth? All other writers had been crushed and overlaid by the enormous weight of facts and documents. Mr Ricardo had deduced, a priori from the understanding itself, laws which first gave a ray of light into the unwieldy chaos of materials, and had constructed what had been but a collection of tentative discussions into a science of regular proportions, now first standing on an eternal basis.

Thus did one single work of a profound understanding avail to give me a pleasure and an activity which I had not known for years. It roused me even to write, or, at least, to dictate, what M. wrote for me. It seemed to me that some important truths had escaped even "the inevitable eye"* of Mr Ricardo, and as these were, for the most part, of such a nature that I could express or illustrate them more briefly and elegantly by algebraic symbols than in the usual clumsy and loitering diction of economists, the whole would not have filled a pocketbook. And being so brief, with M. for my amanuensis, even at this time incapable as I was of all general exertion, I drew up my *Prolegomena to all Future Systems of Political Economy*.* I hope it will not be found redolent of opium – though, indeed, to most people the subject itself is a sufficient opiate.

This exertion, however, was but a temporary flash, as the sequel showed, for I designed to publish my work: arrangements were made at a provincial press about eighteen miles distant for printing it. An additional compositor was retained, for some days, on this account. The work was even twice advertised, and I was, in a manner, pledged to the fulfilment of my intention. But I had a preface to write, and a dedication, which I wished to make a splendid one, to Mr Ricardo. I found myself quite unable to accomplish all this. The arrangements were countermanded, the compositor dismissed and my *Prolegomena* rested peacefully by the side of its elder and more dignified brother.

I have thus described and illustrated my intellectual torpor in terms that apply, more or less, to every part of the four years during which I was under the Circean* spells of opium. But for misery and suffering, I might, indeed, be said to have existed in a dormant state. I seldom could prevail on myself to write a letter: an answer of a few words, to any that I received, was the utmost that I could accomplish, and often *that* not until the letter had lain weeks or even months on my writing table. Without the aid of M., all records of bills paid or *to be* paid must have perished, and my whole domestic economy, whatever became of political economy, must have gone into irretrievable confusion. I shall not afterwards allude to this part of the case. It is one, however, which the opium-eater will find, in the end, as oppressive and tormenting as any other, from the sense of incapacity and feebleness, from the direct embarrassments incident to the neglect or procrastination of each day's appropriate duties and from the remorse which must often exasperate the stings of these evils to a reflective and conscientious mind. The opium-eater loses none of his moral sensibilities or aspirations: he wishes and longs, as earnestly as ever, to realize what he believes possible and feels to be exacted by duty, but his intellectual apprehension of what is possible infinitely outruns his power – not of execution only, but even of power to attempt. He lies under the weight of incubus and nightmare; he lies in sight of all that he would fain perform, just as a man forcibly confined to his bed by the mortal languor of a relaxing disease, who is compelled to witness injury or outrage offered to some object of his tenderest love; he curses the spells which chain him down from motion; he would lay down his life if he might but get up and walk, but he is powerless as an infant, and cannot even attempt to rise.

I now pass to what is the main subject of these latter confessions, to the history and journal of what took place in my dreams, for these were the immediate and proximate cause of my acutest suffering.

The first notice I had of any important change going on in this part of my physical economy was from the reawakening of a state of eye generally incident to childhood or exalted states of irritability. I know not whether my reader is aware that many children, perhaps most, have a power of painting, as it were, upon the darkness all sorts of phantoms. In some, that power is simply a mechanic affection of the eye; others have a voluntary or a semi-voluntary power to dismiss or to summon them, or, as a child once said to me when I questioned him on this matter, "I can tell them to go, and they go, but sometimes they come when I don't tell them to come." Whereupon I told him that he had almost as unlimited a command over apparitions as a Roman centurion over his soldiers.* In the middle of 1817 I think it was that this faculty became positively distressing to me. At night, when I lay awake in bed, vast processions passed along in mournful pomp – friezes of never-ending stories that to my feelings were as sad and solemn as if they were stories drawn from times before Oedipus or Priam, before Tyre, before Memphis.* And, at the same time, a corresponding change took place in my dreams: a theatre seemed suddenly opened and lighted up within my brain, which presented nightly spectacles of more than earthly splendour. And the four following facts may be mentioned as noticeable at this time:

1. That as the creative state of the eye increased, a sympathy seemed to arise between the waking and the dreaming states of the brain in one point: that whatsoever I happened to call up and to trace by a voluntary act upon the darkness was very apt to transfer itself to my dreams, so that I feared to exercise this faculty, for as Midas turned all things to gold, that yet baffled his hopes and defrauded his human desires, so whatsoever things capable of being visually represented I did but think of in the darkness

immediately shaped themselves into phantoms of the eye – and, by a process apparently no less inevitable, when thus once traced in faint and visionary colours, like writings in sympathetic ink,* they were drawn out by the fierce chemistry of my dreams into insufferable splendour that fretted my heart.

2. For this and all other changes in my dreams were accompanied by deep-seated anxiety and gloomy melancholy, such as are wholly incommunicable by words. I seemed every night to descend, not metaphorically, but literally to descend into chasms and sunless abysses, depths below depths, from which it seemed hopeless that I could ever reascend. Nor did I, by waking, feel that I *had* reascended. This I do not dwell upon, because the state of gloom which attended these gorgeous spectacles, amounting at last to utter darkness, as of some suicidal despondency, cannot be approached by words.

3. The sense of space and, in the end, the sense of time were both powerfully affected. Buildings, landscapes, etc., were exhibited in proportions so vast as the bodily eye is not fitted to receive. Space swelled and was amplified to an extent of unutterable infinity. This, however, did not disturb me so much as the vast expansion of time. I sometimes seemed to have lived for seventy or one hundred years in one night. Nay, sometimes had feelings representative of a millennium passed in that time – or, however, of a duration far beyond the limits of any human experience.

4. The minutest incidents of childhood, or forgotten scenes of later years, were often revived. I could not be said to recollect them, for if I had been told of them when waking, I should not have been able to acknowledge them as parts of my past experience. But placed as they were before me, in dreams like intuitions, and clothed in all their evanescent

circumstances and accompanying feelings, I *recognized* them instantaneously. I was once told by a near relative of mine* that, having in her childhood fallen into a river and being on the very verge of death but for the critical assistance which reached her, she saw in a moment her whole life, in its minutest incidents, arrayed before her simultaneously as in a mirror, and she had a faculty developed as suddenly for comprehending the whole and every part. This, from some opium experiences of mine, I can believe. I have, indeed, seen the same thing asserted twice in modern books, and accompanied by a remark which I am convinced is true; viz. that the dread book of account which the Scriptures speak of* is, in fact, the mind itself of each individual. Of this, at least, I feel assured: that there is no such thing as *forgetting* possible to the mind. A thousand accidents may and will interpose a veil between our present consciousness and the secret inscriptions on the mind – accidents of the same sort will also rend away this veil – but alike, whether veiled or unveiled, the inscription remains for ever, just as the stars seem to withdraw before the common light of day, whereas in fact we all know that it is the light which is drawn over them as a veil, and that they are waiting to be revealed when the obscuring daylight shall have withdrawn.

Having noticed these four facts as memorably distinguishing my dreams from those of health, I shall now cite a case illustrative of the first fact, and shall then cite any others that I remember, either in their chronological order or any other that may give them more effect as pictures to the reader.

I had been in youth – and even since, for occasional amusement – a great reader of Livy,* whom I confess that I prefer, both for style and matter, to any other of the Roman historians, and I had often felt as most solemn and appalling sounds, and most emphatically representative of the majesty of the

Roman people, the two words so often occurring in Livy – *Consul Romanus* – especially when the consul is introduced in his military character. I mean to say that the words king, sultan, regent, etc., or any other titles of those who embody in their own persons the collective majesty of a great people, had less power over my reverential feelings. I had also, though no great reader of history, made myself minutely and critically familiar with one period of English history, viz. the period of the Parliamentary War, having been attracted by the moral grandeur of some who figured in that day, and by the many interesting memoirs which survive those unquiet times. Both these parts of my lighter reading, having furnished me often with matter of reflection, now furnished me with matter for my dreams. Often I used to see, after painting upon the blank darkness a sort of rehearsal whilst waking, a crowd of ladies, and perhaps a festival and dances. And I heard it said, or I said to myself, "These are English ladies from the unhappy times of Charles I. These are the wives and the daughters of those who met in peace and sat at the same tables and were allied by marriage or by blood, and yet, after a certain day in August 1642, never smiled upon each other again, nor met but in the field of battle – and at Marston Moor, at Newbury or at Naseby* cut asunder all ties of love by the cruel sabre and washed away in blood the memory of ancient friendship." The ladies danced and looked as lovely as the court of George IV.* Yet I knew, even in my dream, that they had been in the grave for nearly two centuries. This pageant would suddenly dissolve, and at a clapping of hands would be heard the heart-quaking sound of "*Consul Romanus*", and immediately came "sweeping by" in gorgeous paludaments Paullus or Marius, girt round by a company of centurions, with the crimson tunic hoisted on a spear, and followed by the *alalagmos* of the Roman legions.*

Many years ago, when I was looking over Piranesi's *Antiquities of Rome*,* Mr Coleridge, who was standing by, described to me a set of plates by that artist, called his *Dreams*, and which record the scenery of his own visions during the delirium of a fever. Some of them (I describe only from memory of Mr Coleridge's account) represented vast Gothic halls, on the floor of which stood all sorts of engines and machinery, wheels, cables, pulleys, levers, catapults, etc., etc., expressive of enormous power put forth and resistance overcome. Creeping along the sides of the walls you perceived a staircase – and upon it, groping his way upwards, was Piranesi himself. Follow the stairs a little farther and you perceive it come to a sudden abrupt termination, without any balustrade, and allowing no step onwards to him who had reached the extremity except into the depths below. Whatever is to become of poor Piranesi, you suppose, at least, that his labours must in some way terminate here. But raise your eyes and behold a second flight of stairs still higher, on which again Piranesi is perceived, but this time standing on the very brink of the abyss. Again elevate your eye, and a still more aerial flight of stairs is beheld, and again is poor Piranesi busy on his aspiring labours, and so on until the unfinished stairs and Piranesi both are lost in the upper gloom of the hall. With the same power of endless growth and self-reproduction did my architecture proceed in dreams. In the early stage of my malady, the splendours of my dreams were indeed chiefly architectural, and I beheld such pomp of cities and palaces as was never yet beheld by the waking eye, unless in the clouds. From a great modern poet I cite part of a passage which describes, as an appearance actually beheld in the clouds, what in many of its circumstances I saw frequently in sleep:

The appearance, instantaneously disclosed,
Was of a mighty city – boldly say
A wilderness of building, sinking far
And self-withdrawn into a wondrous depth,
Far sinking into splendour – without end!
Fabric it seem'd of diamond and of gold,
With alabaster domes and silver spires,
And blazing terrace upon terrace high
Uplifted: here, serene pavilions bright
In avenues disposed; there, towers begirt
With battlements that on their restless fronts
Bore stars – illumination of all gems!
By earthly nature had the effect been wrought
Upon the dark materials of the storm
Now pacified: on them, and on the coves
And mountain steeps and summits, whereunto
The vapours had receded, taking there
Their station under a cerulean sky.* etc., etc.

The sublime circumstance – "battlements that on their *restless* fronts bore stars" – might have been copied from my architectural dreams, for it often occurred. We hear it reported of Dryden, and of Fuseli* in modern times, that they thought proper to eat raw meat for the sake of obtaining splendid dreams. How much better for such a purpose to have eaten opium, which yet I do not remember that any poet is recorded to have done, except the dramatist Shadwell* – and in ancient days Homer is, I think, rightly reputed to have known the virtues of opium.

To my architecture succeeded dreams of lakes and silvery expanses of water. These haunted me so much that I feared (though possibly it will appear ludicrous to a medical man) that some dropsical state or tendency of the brain might thus be making itself (to use a metaphysical word) *objective*,* and the sentient organ *project* itself as its own object. For two months I suffered greatly in my head – a part of my bodily structure which had hitherto been so clear from all touch or taint of weakness (physically, I mean) that I used to say of it, as the last Lord Orford* said of his stomach, that it seemed likely to survive the rest of my person. Till now I had never felt a headache even, or any the slightest pain, except rheumatic pains caused by my own folly. However, I got over this attack, though it must have been verging on something very dangerous.

The waters now changed their character. From translucent lakes shining like mirrors, they now became seas and oceans. And now came a tremendous change – which, unfolding itself slowly like a scroll, through many months promised an abiding torment. And, in fact, it never left me until the winding up of my case. Hitherto the human face had mixed often in my dreams, but not despotically, nor with any special power of tormenting. But now that which I have called the "tyranny of the human face" began to unfold itself. Perhaps some part of my London life might be answerable for this. Be that as it may, now it was that upon the rocking waters of the ocean the human face began to appear. The sea appeared paved with innumerable faces, upturned to the heavens. Faces, imploring, wrathful, despairing, surged upwards by thousands, by myriads, by generations, by centuries. My agitation was infinite – my mind tossed and surged with the ocean.

* * *

May 1818.

The Malay has been a fearful enemy for months. I have been every night, through his means, transported into Asiatic scenes. I know not whether others share in my feelings on this point, but I have often thought that if I were compelled to forgo England and to live in China, and among Chinese manners and modes of life and scenery, I should go mad. The causes of my horror lie deep, and some of them must be common to others. Southern Asia, in general, is the seat of awful images and associations. As the cradle of the human race, it would alone have a dim and reverential feeling connected with it. But there are other reasons. No man can pretend that the wild, barbarous and capricious superstitions of Africa, or of savage tribes elsewhere, affect him in the way that he is affected by the ancient, monumental, cruel and elaborate religions of Indostan etc. The mere antiquity of Asiatic things, of their institutions, histories, modes of faith, etc. is so impressive that to me the vast age of the race and name overpowers the sense of youth in the individual. A young Chinese seems to me an antediluvian man renewed. Even Englishmen, though not bred in any knowledge of such institutions, cannot but shudder at the mystic sublimity of castes that have flowed apart, and refused to mix, through such immemorial tracts of time – nor can any man fail to be awed by the names of the Ganges or the Euphrates. It contributes much to these feelings that southern Asia is, and has been for thousands of years, the part of the earth most swarming with human life – the great *officina gentium*.* Man is a weed in those regions. The vast empires also, into which the enormous population of Asia has always been cast, give a further sublimity to the feelings associated with all oriental names or images.

In China, over and above what it has in common with the rest of southern Asia, I am terrified by the modes of life, by the manners and the barrier of utter abhorrence and want of sympathy placed between us by feelings deeper than I can analyse. I could sooner live with lunatics or brute animals. All this, and much more than I can say or have time to say, the reader must enter into before he can comprehend the unimaginable horror which these dreams of oriental imagery and mythological tortures impressed upon me. Under the connecting feeling of tropical heat and vertical sun lights, I brought together all creatures, birds, beasts, reptiles, all trees and plants, usages and appearances that are found in all tropical regions, and assembled them together in China or Indostan. From kindred feelings, I soon brought Egypt and all her gods under the same law. I was stared at, hooted at, grinned at, chattered at by monkeys, by parakeets, by cockatoos. I ran into pagodas, and was fixed, for centuries, at the summit or in secret rooms. I was the idol, I was the priest, I was worshipped, I was sacrificed. I fled from the wrath of Brahma through all the forests of Asia. Vishnu hated me, Śiva laid wait for me. I came suddenly upon Isis and Osiris.* I had done a deed, they said, which the ibis and the crocodile trembled at. I was buried, for a thousand years, in stone coffins, with mummies and sphinxes, in narrow chambers at the heart of eternal pyramids. I was kissed, with cancerous kisses, by crocodiles, and laid, confounded with all unutterable slimy things, amongst reeds and Nilotic mud.

I thus give the reader some slight abstraction of my oriental dreams, which always filled me with such amazement at the monstrous scenery that horror seemed absorbed, for a while, in sheer astonishment. Sooner or later came a reflux of feeling that swallowed up the astonishment and left me not so much in terror as in hatred and abomination of what I saw. Over every form and threat and punishment and dim, sightless incarceration, brooded a sense of eternity and infinity that drove me into an oppression as of madness. Into these dreams only it was, with one or two slight exceptions, that any circumstances of physical horror entered. All before had been moral and spiritual terrors. But here the main agents were ugly birds or snakes or crocodiles – especially the last. The cursed crocodile became to me the object of more horror than almost all the rest. I was compelled to live with him, and (as was always the case almost in my dreams) for centuries. I escaped sometimes, and found myself in Chinese houses, with cane tables etc. All the feet of the tables, sofas, etc., soon became instinct with life: the abominable head of the crocodile, and his leering eyes, looked out at me, multiplied into a thousand repetitions, and I stood loathing and fascinated. And so often did this hideous reptile haunt my dreams that many times the very same dream was broken up in the very same way: I heard gentle voices speaking to me (I hear everything when I am sleeping), and instantly I awoke. It was broad noon, and my children were standing, hand in hand, at my bedside, come to show me their coloured shoes or new frocks, or to let me see them dressed for going out. I protest that so awful was the transition from the damned crocodile and the other unutterable monsters and abortions of my dreams to the sight of innocent *human* natures and of infancy that, in the mighty and sudden revulsion of mind, I wept and could not forbear it as I kissed their faces.

* * *

June 1819.

I have had occasion to remark, at various periods of my life, that the deaths of those whom we love, and indeed the contemplation of death generally, is (*cæteris paribus*)* more affecting in summer than in any other season of the year. And the reasons are these three, I think. First, that the visible heavens in summer appear far higher, more distant and (if such a solecism may be excused) more infinite. The clouds, by which chiefly the eye expounds the distance of the blue pavilion stretched over our heads, are in summer more voluminous, massed and accumulated in far grander and more towering piles. Secondly, the light and the appearances of the declining and the setting sun are much more fitted to be types and characters of the infinite. And thirdly (which is the main reason), the exuberant and riotous prodigality of life naturally forces the mind more powerfully upon the antagonist thought of death and the wintry sterility of the grave. For it may be observed, generally, that wherever two thoughts stand related to each other by a law of antagonism and exist, as it were, by mutual repulsion, they are apt to suggest each other. On these accounts it is that I find it impossible to banish the thought of death when I am walking alone in the endless days of summer – and any particular death, if not more affecting, at least haunts my mind more obstinately and besiegingly in that season. Perhaps this cause, and a slight incident which I omit, might have been the immediate occasions of the following dream – to which, however, a predisposition must always have existed in my mind, but having been once roused, it never left me, and split into a thousand fantastic varieties which often suddenly reunited and composed again the original dream.

I thought that it was a Sunday morning in May, that it was Easter Sunday and as yet very early in the morning. I was standing, as it seemed to me, at the door of my own cottage. Right before me lay the very scene which could really be commanded from that situation, but exalted, as was usual, and solemnized by the power of dreams. There were the same mountains and the same lovely valley at their feet, but the mountains were raised to more than Alpine height, and there was interspace far larger between them of meadows and forest lawns. The hedges were rich with white roses, and no living creature was to be seen, excepting that in the green churchyard there were cattle tranquilly reposing upon the verdant graves, and particularly round about the grave of a child whom I had tenderly loved, just as I had really beheld them a little before sunrise in the same summer when that child died.* I gazed upon the well-known scene and I said aloud (as I thought) to myself, "It yet wants much of sunrise – and it is Easter Sunday, and that is the day on which they celebrate the first fruits of resurrection.* I will walk abroad: old griefs shall be forgotten today, for the air is cool and still, and the hills are high and stretch away to heaven, and the forest glades are as quiet as the churchyard, and with the dew I can wash the fever from my forehead, and then I shall be unhappy no longer." And I turned as if to open my garden gate, and immediately I saw upon the left a scene far different, but which yet the power of dreams had reconciled into harmony with the other. The scene was an oriental one, and there also it was Easter Sunday and very early in the morning. And at a vast distance were visible, as a stain upon the horizon, the domes and cupolas of a great city – an image or faint abstraction caught perhaps in childhood from some picture of Jerusalem. And not a bowshot from me, upon a stone, and shaded by Judean palms, there sat a woman – and I looked, and it was... Ann! She fixed her eyes upon me earnestly, and I said to her at length, "So then I have found you, at last." I waited, but she answered me not a word. Her face was the same as when I saw it last, and yet again how different! Seventeen years ago, when the lamplight fell upon her face as for the last time I kissed her lips (lips, Ann, that to me were not polluted), her eyes were streaming with tears. The tears were now wiped away: she seemed more beautiful than she was at that time, but in all other points the same, and not older. Her looks were tranquil, but with unusual solemnity of expression, and I now gazed upon her with some awe, but suddenly her countenance grew dim – and, turning to the mountains, I perceived vapours rolling between us. In a moment all had vanished: thick darkness came on, and, in the twinkling of an eye,* I was far away from mountains, and by lamplight in Oxford Street, walking again with Ann, just as we walked seventeen years before when we were both children.

As a final specimen, I cite one of a different character, from 1820.

The dream commenced with a music which now I often heard in dreams – a music of preparation and of awakening suspense – a music like the opening of the Coronation Anthem,* and which, like *that*, gave the feeling of a vast march, of infinite cavalcades filing off and the tread of innumerable armies. The morning was come of a mighty day – a day of crisis and of final hope for human nature, then suffering some mysterious eclipse and labouring in some dread extremity. Somewhere, I knew not where – somehow, I knew not how – by some beings, I knew not whom – a battle, a strife, an agony, was conducting – was evolving like a great drama or piece of music – with which my sympathy was the more insupportable from my confusion as to its place, its cause, its nature and its possible issue. I, as is usual in dreams (where of necessity we make ourselves central to every movement), had the power, and yet had not the power, to decide it. I had the power, if I could raise myself, to will it, and yet again had not the power, for the weight of twenty Atlantics was upon me, or the oppression of inexpiable guilt. "Deeper than ever plummet sounded",* I lay inactive. Then, like a chorus, the passion deepened. Some greater interest was at stake – some mightier cause than ever yet the sword had pleaded or trumpet had proclaimed. Then came sudden alarms, hurryings to and fro: trepidations of innumerable fugitives, I knew not whether from the good cause or the bad, darkness and lights, tempest and human faces – and at last, with the sense that all was lost, female forms, and the features that were worth all the world to me, and but a moment allowed – and clasped hands, and heartbreaking partings, and then... everlasting farewells! And with a sigh, such as the caves of hell sighed when the incestuous mother uttered the abhorred name of death,* the sound was reverberated – everlasting farewells! And again, and yet again reverberated – everlasting farewells!

And I awoke in struggles and cried aloud, "I will sleep no more!"*

But I am now called upon to wind up a narrative which has already extended to an unreasonable length. Within more spacious limits, the materials which I have used might have been better unfolded, and much which I have not used might have been added with effect. Perhaps, however, enough has been given. It now remains that I should say something of the way in which this conflict of horrors was finally brought to its crisis. The reader is already aware (from a passage near the beginning of the introduction to the first part) that the

Opium-Eater has, in some way or other, "unwound, almost to its final links, the accursed chain which bound him".* By what means? To have narrated this, according to the original intention, would have far exceeded the space which can now be allowed. It is fortunate, as such a cogent reason exists for abridging it, that I should, on a maturer view of the case, have been exceedingly unwilling to injure, by any such unaffecting details, the impression of the history itself as an appeal to the prudence and the conscience of the yet unconfirmed Opium-Eater – or even (though a very inferior consideration) to injure its effect as a composition. The interest of the judicious reader will not attach itself chiefly to the subject of the fascinating spells, but to the fascinating power. Not the Opium-Eater, but the opium is the true hero of the tale and the legitimate centre on which the interest revolves. The object was to display the marvellous agency of opium, whether for pleasure or for pain. If that is done, the action of the piece has closed.

However, as some people, in spite of all laws to the contrary, will persist in asking what became of the Opium-Eater, and in what state he now is, I answer for him thus: the reader is aware that opium had long ceased to found its empire on spells of pleasure: it was solely by the tortures connected with the attempt to abjure it that it kept its hold. Yet, as other tortures, no less it may be thought, attended the non-abjuration of such a tyrant, a choice only of evils was left, and *that* might as well have been adopted which, however terrific in itself, held out a prospect of final restoration to happiness. This appears true, but good logic gave the author no strength to act upon it. However, a crisis arrived for the author's life, and a crisis for other objects still dearer to him – and which will always be far dearer to him than his life, even now that it is again a happy one. I saw that I must die if I continued the opium. I determined, therefore, if that should be required, to die in throwing it off. How much I was at that time taking I cannot say, for the opium which I used had been purchased for me by a friend who afterwards refused to let me pay him, so that I could not ascertain even what quantity I had used within the year. I apprehend, however, that I took it very irregularly, and that I varied from about fifty or sixty grains to 150 a day. My first task was to reduce it to forty, to thirty and, as fast as I could, to twelve grains.

I triumphed, but think not, reader, that therefore my sufferings were ended – nor think of me as of one sitting in a *dejected* state. Think of me as of one, even when four months had passed, still agitated, writhing, throbbing, palpitating, shattered and much, perhaps, in the situation of him who has been racked, as I collect the torments of that state from the affecting account of them left by a most innocent sufferer* (of the times of James I). Meantime, I derived no benefit from any medicine except one prescribed to me by an Edinburgh surgeon of great eminence, viz. ammoniated tincture of valerian.* Medical account, therefore, of my emancipation I have not much to give, and even that little, as managed by a man so ignorant of medicine as myself, would probably tend only to mislead. At all events, it would be misplaced in this situation. The moral of the narrative is addressed to the opium-eater, and therefore of necessity limited in its application. If he is taught to fear and tremble, enough has been effected. But he may say that the issue of my case is at least a proof that opium, after a seventeen years' use and an eight years' abuse of its powers, may still be renounced, and that *he* may chance to bring to the task greater energy than I did, or that with a stronger constitution than mine he may obtain the same results with less.

This may be true. I would not presume to measure the efforts of other men by my own. I heartily wish him more energy. I wish him the same success. Nevertheless, I had motives external to myself which he may unfortunately want, and these supplied me with conscientious supports which mere personal interests might fail to supply to a mind debilitated by opium.

Jeremy Taylor conjectures that it may be as painful to be born as to die.* I think it probable, and, during the whole period of diminishing the opium, I had the torments of a man passing out of one mode of existence into another. The issue was not death, but a sort of physical regeneration, and I may add that ever since, at intervals, I have had a restoration of more than youthful spirits, though under the pressure of difficulties which in a less happy state of mind I should have called misfortunes.

One memorial of my former condition still remains: my dreams are not yet perfectly calm; the dread swell and agitation of the storm have not wholly subsided; the legions that encamped in them are drawing off, but not all departed; my sleep is still tumultuous, and, like the gates of Paradise to our first parents when looking back from afar, it is still (in the tremendous line of Milton)

> With dreadful faces throng'd and fiery arms.*

Note on the Text

Confessions of an English Opium-Eater was first published in *The London Magazine* in two instalments between September and October 1821. It was then republished in book form the following year by the owners of *The London Magazine*, with only a small number of minor revisions. The present edition is based on the original 1821 version, but the spelling and punctuation have been modernized where necessary. It should also be noted that De Quincey expanded the work by more than double its original length for the 1856 edition that appeared in his collected works *Selections Grave and Gay*, and useful additional information gleaned from that version has been used in our footnotes to shed light on the names of people and places withheld in the original. Many thanks to Roger Clarke for his assistance with the ancient Greek quotations.

Notes

p. 3, *decent drapery*: From the author, Whig politician and philosopher Edmund Burke's (*c.*1729–97) *Reflections on the Revolution in France* (1790).

p. 3, *demi-reps*: A term for women whose reputations are only semi-respectable.

p. 3, *French literature... of the French*: A reference, in particular, to the Swiss-born philosopher and writer Jean-Jacques Rousseau (1712–78) and the German poet, playwright, novelist and philosopher Johann Wolfgang von Goethe (1749–1832). The former's *Confessions* (1782–89) is a self-portrayal that does not shrink from laying bare the author's most humiliating and shameful moments. Goethe is referenced primarily for *The Sorrows of Young Werther* (1774), which depicts the emotional turmoil of a young man who is passionately in love with a woman who is betrothed to another.

p. 4, *Humbly... penitential loneliness*: See William Wordsworth's (1770–1850) 'The White Doe of Rylstone' (1815), ll. 176–77.

p. 4, *not yet recorded*: "Not yet recorded" I say, for there is one celebrated man of the present day who, if all be true which is reported of him, has greatly exceeded me in quantity. (DE QUINCEY'S NOTE) The "celebrated man" De Quincey is referring to is, of course, Samuel Taylor Coleridge (1772–1834), whose opium consumption was both prodigious and well known.

p. 5, *eloquent and benevolent* ——*... Mr* ——: References to, in order, the politician and abolitionist William Wilberforce (1759–1833); Dr Isaac Milner (1750–1820), President of Queens' College, Cambridge, and Dean of Carlisle; the lawyer and politician Thomas Erskine (1750–1823), 1st Baron Erskine, who was Lord Chancellor between 1806 and 1807; Coleridge is "the philosopher"; John Hiley Addington (1759–1818) was Under-Secretary of State for Home Affairs between 1812 and 1818; the poet and novelist Charles Lloyd (1775–1839).

p. 6, *a view to suicide*: Opium was a popular means through which to commit suicide.

p. 6, *That those eat now... eat the more*: A remodelling of the poet and clergyman Thomas Parnell's (1679–1718) translation of the Latin poem 'Pervigilium Veneris', which Parnell renders as 'The Vigil of Venus': "Let those love now who never lov'd before; / Let those who always loved now love the more."

p. 7, *Mead*: The physician Richard Mead (1673–1754) devoted an essay in his *A Mechanical Account of Poisons* (1702) to opium.

p. 7, *φωνᾶντα συνετοῖσι*: "That speak to the wise" (Ancient Greek). The quotation is from the Greek lyric poet Pindar's (*c.*520–435 BC) *Olympian Odes*, II, l. 85.

p. 8, *whose talk is of oxen*: From the ancient work of ethical teachings known as the *Book of Ecclesiasticus*, or *The Wisdom of Sirach*: "How can he get wisdom that holdeth the plough, and that glorieth in the goad, that driveth oxen, and is occupied in their labours, and whose talk is of bullocks?"

p. 8, *Humani nihil a se alienum putat*: "He thinks that nothing human is alien to him" (Latin). From Cicero's (106–43 BC) *De officiis*, in which the author adapts a quotation from the Roman dramatist Terence's (*c.*195–159 BC) play *Hautontimorumenos* to suit his purpose.

p. 8, *recent illustrious exception*: A third exception might perhaps have been added, and my reason for not adding that exception is chiefly because it was only in his juvenile efforts that the writer whom I allude to expressly addressed himself to philosophical themes; his riper powers having been all dedicated (on very excusable and very intelligible grounds, under the present direction of the popular mind in England) to criticism and the fine arts. This reason apart, however, I doubt whether he is not rather to be considered an acute thinker than a subtle one. It is, besides, a great drawback on his mastery over philosophical subjects that he has obviously not had the advantage of a regular scholastic education: he has not read Plato in his youth (which most likely was only his misfortune), but neither has he read Kant in his manhood (which is his fault). (DE QUINCEY'S NOTE) The note concerns the essayist, philosopher and critic William Hazlitt (1778–1830).

p. 8, *David Ricardo*: The political economist David Ricardo (1772–1823).

p. 9, *Scottish professors*: I disclaim any allusion to *existing* professors, of whom indeed I know only one. (DE QUINCEY'S NOTE) The one De Quincey knew was his friend John Wilson (1785–1854), the author and critic who wrote for *Blackwood's Edinburgh Magazine* and was a fellow Lake District resident and acolyte of William Wordsworth's. The comment about Scottish professors appears primarily to be a denouncement of Dugald Stewart (1753–1828), perhaps the most famous living philosopher in Britain at the time. Richard Woodhouse (1788–1834), the lawyer and writer best known for his friendship with John Keats (1795–1821), reported that De Quincey said, in reference to Stewart, that he had "no originality or grasp of mind in him" and that all his "disquisitions are little, and the subject of them of no moment".

p. 10, *four guardians*: The merchant Thomas Belcher, the magistrate James Entwhistle, the banker Henry Gee and the clergyman Samuel Hall.

p. 10, *one of my masters*: The Reverend Nathaniel Morgan, master of Bath Grammar School.

p. 10, *and a ripe and good one*: From Shakespeare's *Henry VIII* (Act IV, Sc. 2, l. 51): "He was a scholar, and a ripe and good one".

p. 10, *blockhead*: The Revered Edward Spencer, headmaster of Spencer's Academy, Wingfield.

p. 10, *respectable scholar... ancient foundation*: Charles Lawson, high master of Manchester Grammar School, which was founded in 1515.

p. 10, —— *College, Oxford*: Brasenose College, Oxford.

p. 11, *sacrifice to the Graces*: The Graces were the attendants of Aphrodite and were associated with beauty and charm.

To sacrifice to the Graces therefore means to conduct oneself courteously and with charm.

p. 11, *archididascalus*: Headmaster. A compound word made up of *archi* ("chief") and *didascalus* ("teacher").

p. 11, *One, who was more reasonable... opposition to his will*: Henry Gee is the guardian that De Quincey believed to be "more reasonable". The Reverend Samuel Hall is the guardian mentioned less favourably here.

p. 12, *a woman of high rank*: Susan, Lady Carbery (d. 1828). She was a family friend of the De Quinceys and had been left her fortune by Colonel Henry Watson (1737–86), her father. She had then married George Evans, 4th Baron Carbery (1766–1804), in 1792.

p. 12, *double letter*: A letter written on two sheets and charged double postage.

p. 12, *It is a remark of Dr Johnson's... sadness of heart*: A sentiment expressed by Dr Johnson (1709–84) in the 103rd and last of the essays known as *The Idler*.

p. 13, *ancient towers of ——*: The Church of St Mary, which is now Manchester Cathedral.

p. 13, *dressed in earliest light*: From Percy Bysshe Shelley's (1792–1822) *The Revolt of Islam* (1818), V, xliii, ll. 7–8.

p. 14, *pensive citadel*: From Wordsworth's 'Nuns Fret Not at Their Convent's Narrow Room' (1807), l. 3.

p. 14, *a picture of the lovely ——*: Sarah Seymour (1631–92), the dowager Duchess of Somerset, who in the late seventeenth century had given three manors towards the provision of scholarships to Brasenose College, Oxford, and St John's College, Cambridge.

p. 15, *Of Atlantean shoulders... mightiest monarchies*: See John Milton's (1608–74) *Paradise Lost* (1667), II, ll. 306–7.

p. 16, *Seven Sleepers*: A reference to the Seven Sleepers of Ephesus, who were accused by the Emperor Decius

(r. 249–51) of being Christians. They were ordered to recant, but instead went to a cave to pray, after which they fell asleep. The Emperor had them sealed in, and roughly two centuries later, during the reign of Theodosius II (408–50), by which time Christianity had become the state religion of the Roman Empire, the cave was opened and they awoke, believing they had slept for only a single day.

p. 16, *étourderie*: Carelessness.

p. 16, *with Providence my guide*: From *Paradise Lost*, XII, ll. 646–47.

p. 16, *favourite English poet*: Wordsworth.

p. 16, *12mo*: Duodecimo.

p. 16, *other personal accounts*: De Quincey wished to meet William Wordsworth.

p. 16, *Denbighshire, Merionethshire and Caernarvonshire*: Merionethshire is one of the historic counties of Wales. It is situated in the north of the country. Caernarfonshire, spelt Caernarvonshire until the twentieth century, borders Merionethshire to the north.

p. 16, *B——*: Bangor.

p. 17, *Not to know... one's self unknown*: A slight adaptation from *Paradise Lost*, IV, l. 830: "Not to know me argues yourselves unknown".

p. 17, *noli me tangere*: "Touch me not" (Latin). Christ's words to Mary Magdalene following the resurrection.

p. 17, *οἱ πολλοί*: "The many" (ancient Greek). It is the phrase from which "hoi polloi" derives.

p. 18, *Bishop of ——*: William Cleaver, Principal of Brasenose College, Oxford, and the bishop, over the course of his life, of Chester, Bangor and St Asaph.

p. 18, *high road to the Head*: Holyhead, in Anglesey, one of the principal sea ports serving Ireland.

p. 20, *haws*: the fruit of the hawthorn.

p. 20, *Llan-y-styndw (or some such name)*: Perhaps Llanystumdwy in Gwynedd.

p. 21, *gentle blood*: A common phrase; perhaps De Quincey had in mind one of Shakespeare's numerous uses of it, or perhaps Wordsworth's poem 'O Flower of All That Springs from Gentle Blood'.

p. 22, *sapphics or alcaics*: Poems written in sapphic or alcaic metre and named after the poets Sappho and Alcaeus respectively, both of whom are thought to have been born in Lesbos in the seventh century BC.

p. 22, *Mr Shelley… notions about old age*: A reference to Shelley's *The Revolt of Islam*, II, xxxiii, ll. 1–8: "old age… cannot dare / To burst the chains which life forever flings… So is it cold and cruel, and is made / The careless slave of that dark power which brings / Evil, like blight, on man, who, still betrayed, / Laughs o'er the grave in which his living hopes are laid."

p. 23, *hunger-bitten*: Perhaps a reference to Wordsworth's *The Prelude*, IX, ll. 515–16: "we chanced / One day to meet a hunger-bitten girl". The phrase comes from Job 18:12.

p. 24, *the plan of Cromwell*: Oliver Cromwell (1599–1658) was apparently in the habit, as a means of defence and subterfuge, of frequently changing the abode in which he slept.

p. 24, *esculent*: Edible.

p. 25, *Bluebeard room*: In Charles Perrault's (1628–1703) version of the Bluebeard tale, Bluebeard marries a succession of beautiful women, who then subsequently disappear. He informs his new wife that she is allowed anywhere in the castle except for one room. Overcome with curiosity, she enters the room, only to find the corpses of his previous wives.

p. 25, *Tartarus*: The lowest part of the underworld.

p. 26, *laying down*: To relinquish or give up.

p. 26, *cycle and epicycle, orb in orb*: *Paradise Lost*, VIII, l. 84.

p. 26, *Dr Johnson... wall-fruit as he could eat*: The diarist Hester Thrale (1741–1821) recorded this statement of Dr Johnson's in her *Anecdotes of the Late Samuel Johnson* (1786).

p. 26, *the world was all before us*: A slight adaptation of *Paradise Lost*, XII, l. 646: "The world was all before them".

p. 27, *house... conspicuous situation and in a well-known part of London*: De Quincey later noted that it was in Greek Street, on the side nearest to Soho Square.

p. 28, *Sine Cerere*: From Terence's *Eunuchus*, Act IV, Sc. v, l. 6: "*Sine Cerere et Libero friget Venus*" ("Without Ceres and Bacchus, Venus grows cold", Latin). The gods here are representatives of bread, wine and love respectively.

p. 28, *more Socratico*: "In the manner of Socrates" (Latin).

p. 28, *Catholic*: Universal.

p. 31, *to chase, to haunt, to waylay*: Reminiscent of Wordsworth's 'She Was a Phantom of Delight', ll. 9–10: "A dancing shape, an image gay, / To haunt, to startle and waylay".

p. 31, *too deep for tears*: From Wordsworth's 'Ode: Intimations of Immortality from Recollections of Early Childhood' (1807), l. 208.

p. 32, *His late Majesty's*: George III (1738–1820).

p. 32, *l.*: Pound (from the Latin *libra*).

p. 33, *Jew named D——*: To this same Jew, by the way, some eighteen months afterwards, I applied again on the same business, and, dating at that time from a respectable college, I was fortunate enough to gain his serious attention to my proposals. My necessities had not arisen from any extravagance or youthful levities (these my habits and the nature of my pleasures raised me far above), but simply from the vindictive malice of my guardian, who, when he found himself no longer able to prevent me from going to the university, had, as a parting token of his good nature, refused to sign an order for granting me a shilling beyond the allowance made to me at school – viz. 100*l*. per ann. Upon this sum it was, in my time, barely possible to have lived in college, and not possible to a man who, though above the paltry affectation of ostentatious disregard for money, and without any expensive tastes, confided nevertheless rather too much in servants and did not delight in the petty details of minute economy. I soon, therefore, became embarrassed, and at length, after a most voluminous negotiation with the Jew (some parts of which, if I had leisure to rehearse them, would greatly amuse my readers), I was put in possession of the sum I asked for – on the "regular" terms of paying the Jew seventeen and a half per cent by way of annuity on all the money furnished; Israel, on his part, graciously resuming no more than about ninety guineas of the said money, on account of an attorney's bill (for what services, to whom rendered and when, whether at the Siege of Jerusalem, at the building of the Second Temple or on some earlier occasion, I have not yet been able to discover). How many perches this bill measured I really forget, but I still keep it in a cabinet of natural curiosities, and some time or other I believe I shall present it to the British Museum. (DE QUINCEY'S NOTE) De Quincey subsequently named the moneylender as a Mr Dell. The Siege of Jerusalem occurred in AD 70 during the First Roman-Jewish War, while the Second Temple was dedicated in 515 BC. A perch is a measure of length equating to sixteen and a half feet.

p. 33, *Doctors' Commons*: A society of doctors of civil law. Formed in 1509, it once had its premises in Paternoster Row, but moved to Knightrider Street in 1568.

p. 34, *materialiter... formaliter*: "Materially" and "formally" respectively (Latin).

p. 34, *Earl of ——... Marquess of ——*: References to Howe Browne (1788–1845), who became Marquess of Sligo in 1809, but before that was the Earl of Altamont. His father was John Browne, who was the Marquess of Sligo between 1800 and his death in 1809.

p. 34, *M—— and Sl——*: Mayo and Sligo.

p. 37, *fine fluent motion of this mail*: The Bristol mail is the best appointed in the kingdom, owing to the double advantage of an unusually good road and of an extra sum for expenses subscribed by the Bristol merchants. (DE QUINCEY'S NOTE)

p. 39, *Roman poet*: The satirical poet Juvenal said in his *Satires*, X, l. 22: "The empty-pocketed traveller will sing in the robber's face".

p. 39, *a murder committed... in that neighbourhood*: John Cole Steele was murdered on Hounslow Heath in November 1802 – a matter of months before De Quincey found himself there. Steele had left his home in London in order to visit his lavender plantation in Feltham, near Hounslow. The murder horrified the public and was much discussed.

p. 39, *Lord of my learning and no land beside*: Slightly adapted from Shakespeare's *King John*, Act I, Sc. I, l. 138: "Lord of thy presence and no land beside".

p. 39, *Lord ——*: Lord Altamont.

p. 39, *dislike to bullets considerably sharpened*: It will be objected that many men of the highest rank and wealth have in our own day, as well as throughout our history, been amongst the foremost in courting danger in battle. True, but this is not the case supposed: long familiarity with power has to them deadened its effect and its attractions. (DE QUINCEY'S NOTE)

p. 40, *To slacken Virtue... merit praise*: Altered slightly from Milton's *Paradise Regained*, II, ll. 455–56, with "tempt" replacing Milton's "prompt".

p. 40, *Pote's*: Joseph Pote (*c.*1703–87) was a bookseller and publisher in Eton and also ran a boarding house for Eton boys.

p. 40, *University of ——*: University of Cambridge.

p. 40, *Ibi omnis effusus labor*: "Thereupon all his labour was lost" (Latin). From Virgil's *Georgics*, IV, ll. 491–92.

p. 41, *Earl of D——*: John Otway Cuffe (1788–1820), who became Earl of Desart in 1804.

p. 41, *an author*: Thomas Quincey wrote *A Short Tour in the Midland Counties of England, Performed in the Summer of 1772; Together with an Account of a Similar Excursion Undertaken September 1774* (1775).

p. 41, *mother English*: From Coleridge's *Biographia Literaria* (1817).

p. 41, *Lady M.W. Montagu*: The essayist, poet and letter writer Lady Mary Wortley Montagu (1689–1762), who was one of the most colourful and well-known figures of the eighteenth century. Her masterpiece is widely considered to be her fifty-two Turkish Embassy letters, written while her husband was ambassador in Constantinople, which describe many scenes and customs previously unknown to Europeans.

p. 42, *good man's table*: A reworking of *As You Like It*, Act II, Sc. 7, l. 115: "If ever sat at any good man's feast".

p. 42, *story about Otway*: The Restoration playwright Thomas Otway (1652–85), who had fallen on hard times, is said to have bought a roll from a baker's shop after a gentleman gave him a guinea. Otway, ravenous with hunger, choked on the roll and died.

p. 43, *some of his relatives*: John Otway Cuffe's mother was Lady Anne Browne, the sister of the aforementioned John

Browne, Marquess of Sligo (see second note to p. 34). Howe Browne and John Otway Cuffe were therefore cousins.

p. 45, —— *in* ——*shire*: St John's Priory in Cheshire.

p. 45, *myriad*: Ten thousand.

p. 45, *magdalen*: A term used for both repentant female sinners and reformed prostitutes.

p. 47, ——... *fly for comfort*: De Quincey is thinking of Dove Cottage, Wordsworth's home in Grasmere. It was later to be De Quincey's home for eleven years, between 1809 and 1820. De Quincey is also echoing Psalms 55:6: "And I said oh that I had wings like a dove! For then would I fly away and be at rest."

p. 47, *Orestes*: In Greek mythology, the son of Agamemnon and Clytemnestra. In the Homeric version of the myth, Orestes is not present when his father returns from the Trojan War and is murdered by Clytemnestra's lover Aegisthus. Orestes returns seven years later and avenges his father by murdering his mother and Aegisthus. In the final play of Aeschylus's *Oresteia*, *The Eumenides*, Orestes is pursued by the Furies, often known as the Eumenides ("kindly ones") or the Erinyes. In Euripides's play *Orestes*, the eponymous hero is still suffering from the wrath of the Furies, and he is condemned to death for the murder. He is finally saved, however, by Apollo.

p. 47, *blessed*: Φίλον ὕπνου θέλγητρον, ἐπίκουρον νόσου. (DE QUINCEY'S NOTE) "Precious enchantment of sleep, ally against sickness" (Greek). The quotation is from Euripides's *Orestes*, l. 211.

p. 47, *M.*: Margaret De Quincey (née Simpson), whom Thomas married in 1817.

p. 48, *servile*: Τὸ δούλευμ' ἡδύ. *Eurip. Orest.* (DE QUINCEY'S NOTE) "The service is sweet" (Greek). The quotation is from Euripides's *Orestes*, l. 221.

p. 48, *king of men*: Ἄναξ ἀνδρῶν Ἀγαμέμνων. (DE QUINCEY'S NOTE) "Agamemnon, lord of men" (Greek).

p. 48, *hid her face*: Ὄμμα θεῖσ' ἔσω πέπλων. The scholar will know that throughout this passage I refer to the early scenes of the *Orestes* – one of the most beautiful exhibitions of the domestic affections which even the dramas of Euripides can furnish. To the English reader, it may be necessary to say that the situation at the opening of the drama is that of a brother attended only by his sister during the demoniacal possession of a suffering conscience (or, in the mythology of the play, haunted by the Furies), and in circumstances of immediate danger from enemies, and of desertion or cold regard from nominal friends. (DE QUINCEY'S NOTE) The quotation is inaccurate: Euripides's full line (*Orestes*, l. 280) is: σύγγονε, τί κλαίεις κρᾶτα θεῖσ' ἔσω πέπλων, which means: "Sister, why are you weeping, having put your head inside your robes?" (Greek).

p. 49, *my entrance at college*: Worcester College, Oxford, where De Quincey matriculated in 1803.

p. 50, *duller spectacle... not to show*: A play on the first line of Wordsworth's 'Composed upon Westminster Bridge': "Earth has not anything to show more fair".

p. 50, *the stately Pantheon*: From Wordsworth's 'Power of Music', l. 3. The Pantheon was a place of entertainment opened in 1772 on the south side of Oxford Street. Its site is now occupied by Marks & Spencer's Oxford Street Pantheon branch.

p. 50, *evanesced*: This way of going off the stage of life appears to have been well known in the seventeenth century, but at that time to have been considered a peculiar privilege of blood royal, and by no means to be allowed to druggists. For about the year 1686, a poet of rather ominous name (and who, by the by, did ample justice to his name), viz. Mr

Flatman, in speaking of the death of Charles II, expresses his surprise that any prince should commit so absurd an act as dying, because, says he,

"Kings should disdain to die and only disappear.

"They should abscond, that is, into the other world." (DE QUINCEY'S NOTE) The reference is to the poet Thomas Flatman's (1635–88) 'On the Much Lamented Death of our Late Sovereign Lord King Charles II, of Blessed Memory. A Pindarique Ode', ll. 21–25: "But princes (like the wondrous Enoch) should be free / From Death's unbounded tyranny, / And when their godlike race is run, / And nothing glorious left undone, / Never submit to Fate, but only disappear".

p. 51, *revulsion*: A sudden violent change of feeling.

p. 51, *φάρμακον νηπενθές*: "Drug to cure sorrows" (Greek). From Homer's *Odyssey*, IV, l. 221.

p. 51, *l'Allegro… Il Penseroso*: Companion poems by Milton representing poetic mirth and melancholy respectively.

p. 52, *ex cathedra*: "From the chair" (Latin). In other words, speaking with authority.

p. 52, *satiric author*: Unidentified.

p. 52, *By this time… bankrupts*: Tuesdays and Saturdays were the days on which *The Oxford Gazette* and *The London Gazette* respectively were published. They were, and indeed still are, journals of public record, and thus they record such information as appointments to public offices, lists of corporate and personal insolvencies, etc.

p. 52, *die*: Of this, however, the learned appear latterly to have doubted, for in a pirated edition of Buchan's *Domestic Medicine*, which I once saw in the hands of a farmer's wife who was studying it for the benefit of her health, the doctor was made to say, "Be particularly careful never to take above five-and-twenty ounces of laudanum at once"; the true reading being probably five-and-twenty drops, which are held equal to about one grain of crude opium. (DE QUINCEY'S NOTE) William Buchan's (1729–1805) *Domestic Medicine* was an extremely popular book at the time.

p. 52, *meo periculo*: "At my own risk" (Latin).

p. 54, *ponderibus librata suis*: "Balanced by its own weights" (Latin). The quotation is from Ovid's *Metamorphoses*, I, l. 13.

p. 54, *old gentleman says in Athenaeus... ἐμφανίζουσιν οἵτινες εἰσίν*: "They show themselves for who they are" (Greek). From Athenaeus's *The Deipnosophists*.

p. 54, *majestic intellect*: A quotation from Wordsworth's *The Prelude*, XI, ll. 144–45: "And now all ear, but ever with the heart / Employed, and the majestic intellect".

p. 55, *unscientific*: Amongst the great herd of travellers etc. who show sufficiently by their stupidity that they never held any intercourse with opium, I must caution my reader specially against the brilliant author of *Anastasius*. This gentleman, whose wit would lead one to presume him an opium-eater, has made it impossible to consider him in that character from the grievous misrepresentation which he gives of its effects, at p. 215–17 of Vol. I. Upon consideration, it must appear such to the author himself, for, waiving the errors I have insisted on in the text, which (and others) are adopted in the fullest manner, he will himself admit that an old gentleman "with a snow-white beard" who eats "ample doses of opium" and is yet able to deliver what is meant and received as very weighty counsel on the bad effects of that practice is but an indifferent evidence that opium either kills people prematurely or sends them into a madhouse. But, for my part, I see into this old gentleman and his motives: the fact is, he was enamoured of "the little golden receptacle of the pernicious drug" which Anastasius carried about him, and no way of obtaining it so safe and so feasible occurred as that of frightening its owner out of his wits (which, by the by, are none of the strongest). This commentary throws a new light upon the case and greatly improves it as a story, for the old gentleman's speech, considered as a lecture on pharmacy, is highly absurd, but considered as a hoax on Anastasius, it reads excellently. (DE QUINCEY'S NOTE) Thomas Hope (1769–1831) is the author in question. His novel *Anastasius, or Memoirs of a Greek* (1819) was published anonymously and proved to be extremely popular.

p. 55, *materia medica*: The science of drugs.

p. 55, *one person*: Widely believed to be a reference to John Abernethy (1764–1831), a famous surgeon at St Bartholomew's Hospital, London.

p. 57, *late Duke of ——*: The Duke of Norfolk, Charles Howard (1746–1815).

p. 57, *negus*: Wine mixed with hot water and sweetened with sugar.

p. 58, *Grassini sang at the Opera*: Giuseppina Grassini (1773–1850) was a popular contralto. She performed in London between 1804 and 1806.

p. 58, *Andromache at the tomb of Hector*: In Greek mythology, Andromache was the wife of Hector, the Prince of Troy, who was killed by Achilles. The reference is to her lead role in *Achilles at the Siege of Troy* (1798) by Domenico Cimarosa (1749–1801).

p. 58, *extravaganza on that subject in Twelfth Night*: "If music be the food of love, play on". *Twelfth Night*, Act 1, Sc. 1, l. 1.

p. 58, *Religio Medici of Sir T. Browne*: Part 2, section 9, of Sir Thomas Browne's (1605–82) *Religio Medici* (1642).

p. 59, *Weld... Indian women*: The explorer and writer Isaac Weld (1774–1856) compared the manner in which the Native American women spoke to that of Italian women in his *Travels through the States of North America and the Provinces of Upper and Lower Canada During the Years 1795, 1796 and 1797* (1799).

p. 60, *Marinus in his life of Proclus*: Marinus of Neapolis (fl. 5th century AD) wrote a life of the great Neoplatonist philosopher Proclus (412–85). Marinus succeeded Proclus as head of the Academy on the latter's death.

p. 61, *quartern loaf*: A loaf made of a quarter of flour; a loaf of bread weighing four pounds.

p. 61, *bee... soot of chimneys*: De Quincey later noted that in the "large capacious chimneys of the rustic cottages throughout the Lake District... I often used to hear (though not see) bees... On enquiry, I found that soot (chiefly from wood and peats) was useful in some stage of their wax or honey manufacture".

p. 62, *terræ incognitæ*: "Unknown lands" (Latin).

p. 62, *cave of Trophonius*: The oracle of Trophonius was situated in Lebadea, a city in Boeotia. The god – the deified Trophonius, builder of the temple of Apollo at Delphi – dwelt underground and was approached at night by the consultant, who would usually return from the experience looking melancholy and dejected. It was said that they would then never smile again. To "consult the oracle of Trophonius" has passed into proverbial English as a means of expressing a feeling of gloominess.

p. 63, *L——*: Liverpool. De Quincey was staying in Middle Road, Everton.

p. 63, *Behmenism, quietism*: Behmenism is an adherence to the doctrines taught by the German mystic and philosopher Jakob Böhme (1575–1624). Quietism is a form of religious mysticism based on the teaching of Miguel de Molinos (1628–96), a Spanish priest, in which outward forms of devotion were rejected in favour of passive contemplation.

p. 63, *Sir H. Vane, the younger*: Sir Henry Vane the Younger (1613–62) was a politician, statesman and Governor of the Massachusetts Bay Colony.

p. 63, *O just, subtle and mighty opium*: An evocation of Sir Walter Raleigh's (*c.*1552–1618) *The History of the World* (1614): "O eloquent, just and mighty Death!"

p. 64, *the pangs that tempt the spirit to rebel*: From Wordsworth's *The White Doe of Rylstone*, l. 36.

p. 64, *Wrongs... unavenged*: From Wordsworth's *The Excursion*, III, l. 374.

p. 64, *Phidias and Praxiteles*: Two of the great sculptors of the ancient world.

p. 64, *Hekatómpylos*: An epithet meaning "one hundred gates". It was used for several ancient cities, including the Egyptian Thebes and Qumis, capital of the Parthian Empire.

p. 64, *from the anarchy of dreaming sleep*: *The Excursion*, IV, l. 87.

p. 64, *dishonours of the grave*: Not an uncommon phrase, but Jeremy Taylor (1613–67) is the best known and most influential of those who have used it. It features in both his 'Sermon VII' and 'Sermon VIII'.

p. 65, *bed-makers*: The name once used for those who made the beds and tidied the rooms of the students at Oxford and Cambridge. It was also a byword for an easy woman, hence De Quincey's jocose inclusion among the "still frailer vessels".

p. 65, *tintinnabulous*: Pertaining to bell-ringing.

p. 66, *Kant, Fichte, Schelling, etc.*: The philosophers Immanuel Kant (1724–1804), Johann Gottlieb Fichte (1762–1814) and Friedrich Wilhelm Joseph Schelling (1775–1854) were all key figures of German Idealism.

p. 66, *honi soit qui mal y pense*: "May he be shamed who thinks badly of it" (Anglo-Norman). It is famously the motto of the Order of the Garter.

p. 66, *single female servant... housekeeper*: Richard Woodhouse noted that De Quincey married his housekeeper, which would imply that the housekeeper meant here was Margaret. De Quincey, however, always denied this.

p. 66, *my private fortune*: In this sense, his neighbours are partially correct. De Quincey inherited £2,600 when he turned twenty-one. By 1812, however, much of this had been spent.

p. 66, *esquire... slender pretensions to that distinguished honour*: "Esquire" is a term that has had numerous divergent meanings over the centuries. For example, it has traditionally meant a young man of gentle birth, but also a landed proprietor and a man belonging to the higher order of English gentry. It was also used synonymously with an armiger, which was a person with the right to bear heraldic arms. Whichever meaning De Quincey intended here, as a merchant's son, he would have had no right to the title.

p. 66, *X.Y.Z... Custos Rotulorum*: "X.Y.Z." was the name De Quincey wrote under for *The London Magazine* and *Blackwood's Edinburgh Magazine*. Justice of the Peace was one of the offices which rendered one an esquire. The "Custos Rutolorum", or Keeper of the Rolls, is the principal Justice of the Peace in a county.

p. 66, *in the straw*: In childbed.

p. 66, *particular Madeira*: London Particular was Madeira imported especially for the London market. British merchants also, it is said, added brandy to London Particular Madeira.

p. 67, *Dr Buchan*: William Buchan (see fourth note to p. 52).

p. 67, *very melancholy event*: The death of Wordsworth's daughter Catharine when she was just three years old. De Quincey loved her dearly, and he gave partial vent to his grief in a letter to Dorothy Wordsworth: "Oh, that I could have died for her or with her! Willingly, dear friend, I would have done this."

p. 68, *à force d'ennuyer*: "Through boredom" (French).
p. 68, *pandiculation*: Stretching as a sign of weariness.
p. 69, *eudemonist*: One who believes in eudemonism, a system of ethics which bases moral obligation on the likelihood of actions producing happiness.
p. 69, *cotton trade*: A handsome newsroom, of which I was very politely made free in passing through Manchester by several gentlemen of that place, is called, I think, "The Porch", whence I, who am a stranger in Manchester, inferred that the subscribers meant to profess themselves followers of Zeno. But I have been since assured that this is a mistake. (DE QUINCEY'S NOTE) "Stoics" translates as "men of the porch", and this derives from the porch or portico where Zeno (*c.*334–262 BC) lectured. Zeno founded the Stoic school of philosophers, who were characterized by their belief in remaining indifferent to the vicissitudes of pleasure and pain, good or ill fortune, etc. De Quincey is referring to The Portico Library in Mosley Street, Manchester, which opened in 1806 as a newsroom. It still occupies the same site today.
p. 69, *Eclectic*: A class of ancient philosophers who did not attach themselves to any particular school, but rather selected such doctrines as pleased them.
p. 69, *sweet men... absolution*: This quote does not appear anywhere in Chaucer. Perhaps De Quincey had in mind Chaucer's description of the friar in the General Prologue of *The Canterbury Tales* (1387): "Ful sweetly herde he confession, / And plesant was his absolution."
p. 70, *with a snow-white beard... pernicious drug*: See first note to p. 55.
p. 70, *lustrum*: A period of five years.
p. 71, *eight thousand drops*: I here reckon twenty-five drops of laudanum as equivalent to one grain of opium – which, I believe, is the common estimate. However, as both may

be considered variable quantities (the crude opium varying much in strength, and the tincture still more), I suppose that no infinitesimal accuracy can be had in such a calculation. Teaspoons vary as much in size as opium in strength. Small ones hold about 100 drops, so that 8,000 drops are about eighty times a teaspoonful. The reader sees how much I kept within Dr Buchan's indulgent allowance. (DE QUINCEY'S NOTE)

p. 71, *νυχθήμερον*: "A night and a day" (Greek).

p. 71, *That moveth… at all*: See Wordsworth's 'Resolution and Independence' (1807), l. 77.

p. 72, *young girl born and bred amongst the mountains*: Barbara Lewthwaite, who Wordsworth also mentions in his 'The Pet Lamb' (1800) as a "child of beauty rare".

p. 73, *Adelung's Mithridates*: Johann Christoph Adelung (1732–1806) was a grammarian and linguist who published *Mithridates, oder allgemeine Sprachenkunde* (1806), a comparison and classification of all the known languages of the world at the time.

p. 74, *used to opium*: This, however, is not a necessary conclusion: the varieties of effect produced by opium on different constitutions are infinite. A London magistrate (Harriott's *Struggles through Life*, Vol. III, p. 391, 3rd edition) has recorded that, on the first occasion of his trying laudanum for the gout, he took forty drops, the next night sixty and on the fifth night eighty, without any effect whatever, and this at an advanced age. I have an anecdote from a country surgeon, however, which sinks Mr Harriott's case into a trifle, and in my projected medical treatise on opium, which I will publish provided the College of Surgeons will pay me for enlightening their benighted understandings upon this subject, I will relate it, but it is far too good a story to be published gratis. (DE QUINCEY'S NOTE) The Harriott in question is John Harriott (1745–1817).

p. 74, *a-muck*: See the common accounts in any Eastern traveller or voyager of the frantic excesses committed by Malays who have taken opium or are reduced to desperation by ill luck at gambling. (DE QUINCEY'S NOTE) De Quincey may well be thinking of John Hawkesworth's (*c*.1715–73) *An Account of the Voyages Undertaken by the Order of His Present Majesty for Making Discoveries in the Southern Hemisphere* etc. (1773), in which he states, "These are the people among whom the practice that is called *a mock*, or running a muck, has prevailed for time immemorial. It is well known that to run a muck in the original sense of the word is to get intoxicated with opium and then rush into the street with a drawn weapon and kill whoever comes in the way..." Hawkesworth is speaking about Malays in this passage, and indeed "amok" was first used in English as a term for a frenzied Malay.

p. 74, *intercalary*: A term either indicating a line or stanza inserted at intervals in a work, or something that has been inserted between the original or standard members of a series or a whole. De Quincey's point is that he had a year of happiness amidst a series of melancholy years.

p. 75, *French surgeon... hydrophobia*: Jean-Louis Alibert (1768–1837), dermatologist and personal physician to Louis XVIII and Charles X, inoculated himself with matter from cancer sores. The "English one" was perhaps a Mr White, who, according to Sir James McGrigor (1771–1858), Surgeon-General for the Duke of Wellington's army and later Director-General of the Army Medical Service, inoculated himself with pus taken from the bubo of a plague patient. The third of the list, who inoculated himself against hydrophobia, or rabies, was also called White, and he worked as a surgeon in Brighton. He inoculated himself with the saliva of a rabid dog.

p. 75, *a cottage... coach-house*: From 'The Devil's Thoughts' (1799), l. 33, written by Coleridge and Robert Southey (1774–1843).

p. 76, *And at the doors... Castle of Indolence*: An adapted quotation from James Thomson's (1700–48) *The Castle of Indolence*, I, xliii, ll. 5–9.

p. 76, *Mr ——... like a post*: A reference to Thomas Clarkson (1760–1846), an abolitionist and a key figure in the foundation of the Society for Effecting the Abolition of the Slave Trade. He lived in the Lake District and was a friend of Wordsworth's.

p. 76, *fee-simple*: An estate in land belonging to the owner and their heirs for ever.

p. 76, *St Thomas's Day*: 21st December.

p. 77, *Dr Johnson... Jonas Hanway*: Dr Johnson and the writer and philanthropist Jonas Hanway (1712–86) had a public literary disagreement over tea. The former was an ardent advocate of the beverage, while the latter believed it to be unhealthy. A "*bellum internecinum*" is a war of mutual extermination.

p. 77, *a double debt to pay*: From Oliver Goldsmith's (1728–74) 'The Deserted Village' (1770), l. 229.

p. 77, *a parte ante and a parte post*: "Of the preceding part" and "of the succeeding part" (Latin). Terms denoting time without limit in the past and future.

p. 78, *arms like Aurora's... smiles like Hebe's*: Aurora was the Roman goddess of the dawn, while Hebe was the Greek goddess of youth and spring and the cup-bearer of the gods.

p. 79, *a long farewell to happiness... consolations of sleep*: An evocation of Shakespeare's *Henry VIII*, Act III, Sc. 2, l. 351: "So farewell to the little good you bear me. / Farewell! A long farewell to all my greatness!"

p. 79, *as when some great painter... Revolt of Islam*: From Percy Bysshe Shelley's *The Revolt of Islam*, V, xxiii, ll. 8–9.

p. 81, *in medias res*: "In the middle of things" (Latin).

p. 82, —— *reads vilely... Mrs* ——: The actor John Philip Kemble (1757–1823) and Sarah Siddons (1755–1831), Kemble's sister and the best-known tragic actress of the eighteenth century.

p. 82, *Samson Agonistes... Paradise Regained*: Milton's *Samson Agonistes* (1671) was published with *Paradise Regained* in a single volume.

p. 82, *A young lady... W——'s poems to them*: Sophia Lloyd, the wife of the poet Charles Lloyd (see note to p. 5). As elsewhere, "M." is Margaret and "W——" is Wordsworth.

p. 83, *Spinoza's... De emendatione humani intellectus*: The Dutch-Jewish philosopher Baruch Spinoza's (1632–77) *Tractatus de intellectus emendatione* (1677) was unfinished and published posthumously.

p. 84, *a friend in Edinburgh... Mr Ricardo's book*: *Principles of Political Economy and Taxation* (1817). The Edinburgh friend was John Wilson (see note to p. 9).

p. 84, *Thou art the man*: 2 Samuel 12:7.

p. 84, *I supposed thinking*: The reader must remember what I here mean by "thinking", because else this would be a very presumptuous expression. England, of late, has been rich to excess in fine thinkers, in the departments of creative and combining thought, but there is a sad dearth of masculine thinkers in any analytic path. A Scotchman of eminent name has lately told us that he is obliged to quit even mathematics for want of encouragement. (DE QUINCEY'S NOTE) The "Scotchman" was the physicist and mathematician John Leslie (1766–1832), who wrote, in his *Elements of Geometry, Geometrical Analysis and Plane Trigonometry* (1809), that his "original design was to exhibit... the elements of mathematical science in their full extent... But, after due reflection, I have abandoned that aspiring project.

The publication of abstract works in this country procures neither fame nor emolument, and after having discharged the more pressing obligations which I had contracted, I shall consider my time as more agreeably and perhaps more beneficially employed in pursuing without distraction the labyrinths of physical research."

p. 84, *not in academic bowers... oppressed by mercantile and senatorial cares*: David Ricardo did not attend university, but rather was a member of the Stock Exchange and gained a seat in Parliament in 1818.

p. 85, *the inevitable eye*: A phrase that De Quincey used three times in his oeuvre. Perhaps it is an adaptation of Wordsworth's use of "inevitable ear" in 'When First I Journeyed Hither' (1800).

p. 85, *Prolegomena... Economy*: De Quincey's title was inspired by Immanuel Kant's (1724–1804) *Prolegomena to all Future Metaphysics* (1783).

p. 85, *Circean*: Circe, in Greek mythology, was an enchantress who offered unwary visitors a drink from an enchanted cup. They were then turned into swine.

p. 87, *Whereupon... Roman centurion over his soldiers*: An allusion to Matthew 8:8–9: "The centurion answered and said, Lord, I am not worthy that thou shouldst come under my roof, but speak the word only, and my servant shall be healed. For I am a man under authority, having soldiers under me, and I say to this man, Go, and he goeth; and to another, Come, and he cometh".

p. 87, *Oedipus... Memphis*: Oedipus, in Greek mythology, was the king of Thebes; Priam was the legendary king of Troy during the Trojan War; Tyre, in modern-day Lebanon, was one of the two great cities in Phoenicia; Memphis was the capital of Egypt during the Old Kingdom (*c*.2575–*c*.2130 BC).

p. 88, *sympathetic ink*: The name for any of a number of colourless liquids used as inks which then develop colour on the application of heat or a chemical reagent.

p. 89, *near relative of mine*: De Quincey's mother Elizabeth.

p. 89, *dread book of account... Scriptures speak of*: Revelation 20:12: "And I saw the dead, small and great, stand before God, and the books were opened, and another book was opened, which is the book of life, and the dead were judged out of those things which were written in the books, according to their works".

p. 89, *Livy*: Livy (59/64 BC–17 AD) was one of the great Roman historians and author of the *History of Rome*.

p. 90, *Marston Moor... Newbury... Naseby*: Three of the principal battles of the Civil War, fought in 1644, 1643 and 1645 respectively. All three were Parliamentarian victories.

p. 90, *George IV*: George IV (r. 1820–30) was the reigning monarch when De Quincey's *Confessions of an English Opium-Eater* was published. George had been the Prince Regent between 1811 and 1820 due to George III's fragile mental health.

p. 90, *sweeping by... alalagmos of the Roman legions*: "Sweeping by" is a quotation from Milton's 'Il Penseroso' (l. 98); "paludaments" are military cloaks worn by Roman generals and others of high military standing; Paullus and Marius are Lucius Aemilius Paullus Macedonicus (*c.*229–160 BC) and Gaius Marius (157–86 BC), two of the great Roman generals; the crimson tunic was the signal which announced a day of battle; "alalagmos" was a war cry of the ancient Greeks, but De Quincey defined it as "a word expressing collectively the gathering of the Roman war cries – Alála, alála!"

p. 91, *Piranesi's Antiquities of Rome*: The artist Giovanni Battista Piranesi's (1720–78) *Antichità Romane*.

p. 92, *The appearance... cerulean sky*: *The Excursion*, II, ll. 834–51.

p. 92, *Dryden... Fuseli*: John Dryden (1631–1700) and the painter Henry Fuseli (1741–1825). Where De Quincey obtained his information concerning Dryden is not known, for there is no evidence to suggest that he ate raw meat for the sake of his dreams. There was a story regarding Fuseli, in which he ate raw pork chops so that he might dream his painting *The Nightmare* (1781), but it has no basis in fact.

p. 92, *the dramatist Shadwell*: Thomas Shadwell's (*c.*1642–92) drinking and opium consumption were matters of common knowledge.

p. 93, *objective*: That which belongs or is presented to consciousness, as opposed to consciousness itself.

p. 93, *Lord Orford*: The man of letters Horace Walpole, 4th Earl of Orford (1717–97).

p. 94, *officina gentium*: "Workshop of peoples" (Latin).

p. 95, *Brahma... Osiris*: The first three are Hindu deities, while the latter two are Egyptian.

p. 97, *cæteris paribus*: Literally "the rest being equal" (Latin), but often translated as "all things being equal".

p. 98, *a child... when that child died*: Catharine Wordsworth (see second note to p. 67).

p. 98, *Easter Sunday... first fruits of resurrection*: 1 Corinthians 15:20–21: "But now is Christ risen from the dead and become the first fruits of them that slept. For since by man came death, by man came also the resurrection of the dead".

p. 99, *twinkling of an eye*: 1 Corinthians 15:52.

p. 99, *Coronation Anthem*: George Frederick Handel (1685–1759) wrote *Zadok the Priest* (1727) for the coronation of George II (r. 1727–60). It has been performed at every subsequent British coronation.

p. 100, *Deeper than ever plummet sounded*: *The Tempest*, Act III, Sc. 3, l. 101.

p. 100, *incestuous mother... name of death*: *Paradise Lost*, II, ll. 787–89. In the poem, Sin is Satan's daughter, and Death is their incestuous child.

p. 100, *I will sleep no more*: See *Macbeth*, Act II, Sc. 2, l. 38.

p. 101, *unwound... which bound him*: See p. 5 above.

p. 102, *innocent sufferer*: William Lithgow. His book (*Travels* etc.) is ill and pedantically written, but the account of his own sufferings on the rack at Malaga is overpoweringly affecting. (DE QUINCEY'S NOTE) William Lithgow (*c.*1585–*c.*1645) was an adventurer and writer. He was tortured in Malaga in the belief that he was a spy, and he recorded the ordeal in his book *The Totall Discourse of the Rare Adventures and Painefull Peregrinations of Long Nineteene Yeares Travayles from Scotland to the Most Famous Kingdomes in Europe, Asia and Affrica* (1632).

p. 102, *prescribed to me... tincture of valerian*: The valerian was prescribed by George Bell (1777–1832), who was the official surgeon to George IV in Scotland.

p. 103, *Jeremy Taylor... as painful to be born as to die*: As De Quincey noted in the 1856 edition of *Confessions of an English Opium-Eater*, this was actually a sentiment expressed by the polymath Francis Bacon (1561–1626) in his *Essays Civil and Moral* (1625): "It is as natural to die as to be born, and to a little infant, perhaps, the one is as painful as the other."

p. 103, *With dreadful faces... fiery arms*: *Paradise Lost*, XII, l. 644.

Extra Material

on

Thomas De Quincey's

Confessions of an English Opium-Eater

Thomas De Quincey's Life and Works

Birth and Parents

Thomas Quincey was born in Manchester in 1785, the fourth of Thomas Quincey (1753–93) and his wife Elizabeth Penson's (*c.*1756–1846) eight children. The elder Quincey, a merchant, was a cultured man, whose *Short Tour in the Midland Counties of England* was published in 1774. He was also a founder member of the Manchester Literary and Philosophical Society and an ardent opponent of the slave trade.

Childhood and Death of Elizabeth

Most of the younger Thomas's early childhood, plagued by fragile health, was spent in what was then the rural district of Moss Side. His father, having contracted tuberculosis, sought warmer climes, and the younger Thomas saw little of him thereafter. Thomas's life was thus dominated by his strict and austere mother, whom he described as delighting "not in infancy, nor infancy in her". "Usually mothers defend their own cubs right or wrong," he wrote. "Not so my mother... Did a visitor say some flattering thing of a talent or accomplishment by one or other of us, my mother protested so solemnly against the possibility that we could possess either one or the other that we children held it a point of filial duty to believe ourselves the very scamps and refuse of the universe."

Thomas's elder brother William was so wild and unmanageable that he had been sent away to school in Lincolnshire, and Thomas sought the companionship of his three sisters, Mary, Jane and, in particular, Elizabeth. Thomas and Elizabeth read voraciously together, and in later years Thomas considered himself blessed that "his infant feelings were moulded by the gentlest of sisters". In the summer of 1792, when Thomas was six years old, his beloved Elizabeth contracted meningitis and passed away. He wrote of Elizabeth, many years later, that "where my sister was, there was paradise", and that she had a heart "overflowing, even as mine overflowed, with tenderness – and stung, even as mine was stung, by the necessity of being loved". With a father living in foreign climes and a "freezing" mother, Elizabeth was almost the embodiment of love for the infant Thomas. His memories of her, and the vivid recollection, on the day following her death, of entering the room in which her body lay and kissing "the lips that I should kiss no more" – after which he "slunk, like a guilty thing, with stealthy steps from the room" – suffuse his writing, particularly in the form of resurrection, summer days and breezes bringing death in their wake – and, as will become clear, a "desolating grief", a melancholy and a sense of solitude that remained with him for life. All this, with its concomitant and divergent effects, imbued the young boy with a terrible "misgiving of the heart", prompting him to cry even at that tender age: "Life is Finished! Finished it is!"

Death of Thomas Quincey Senior

Thomas suffered a further blow when his father followed Elizabeth to the grave in July 1793. Yet, death was not accompanied in this instance with the same bitter sting, for the boy's memories of his father were few. As he stated in a letter to Dorothy Wordsworth almost twenty years later, he "had seen too little" of his father "to have much love for him". Upon his death, the elder Thomas fixed a patrimony on his sons, which they would receive when they reached the age of twenty-one. Until then, their financial welfare was placed in the hands of four guardians: the clergyman Samuel Hall, the magistrate James Entwhistle, the merchant Thomas Belcher and the banker Henry Gee.

Schooling in Bath, Wingfield and Manchester

The family moved to Bath in 1796, and Thomas was enrolled at Bath Grammar School (now King Edward's School), where his extraordinary ability in the classics swiftly became evident. It was during this period that the Reverend Nathaniel Morgan, master of the school, famously stated that the young Quincey could "harangue an Athenian mob better than you or I could address an English one". It was also at Bath that Thomas's mother changed the family name to De Quincey, and while she swiftly reverted back to Quincey, Thomas kept the new name for life.

The new school year in the autumn of 1799 saw De Quincey begin life at Spencer's Academy in Wingfield (also known as Winkfield) in Wiltshire. As he makes clear in the *Confessions of an English Opium-Eater*, De Quincey was far from happy at his new school, believing the headmaster to be a "blockhead". During the following summer holidays, De Quincey's mother arranged for him to accompany Howe Browne (at the time Viscount Westport and later Marquess of Sligo) – the son of one of the late Mr Quincey's business associates, John Browne – on a trip to London, Windsor, Dublin and County Mayo, followed by a visit to Lady Susan Carbery at Laxton Hall in Northamptonshire.

Manchester Grammar School, Wales and London

These experiences, which included spending time in the august company of Lord Castlereagh, Lord Cornwallis, Lord Clare and even King George III, must have naturally fed the egotism of a boy who already believed himself to be superior in learning to his tutors. De Quincey had no desire to return to Wingfield, and he requested that his education continue at Bath Grammar School. His mother, however, decided that he should be enrolled at Manchester Grammar School, where he was expected to remain for three years. As well as completing his schooling, this would also make him eligible for Manchester Grammar's scholarship to Brasenose College, Oxford. But De Quincey was once again dissatisfied with life at school. He had exchanged the "glittering halls of the English nobility" for the "rude benches of an antique schoolroom". Moreover, Charles Lawson, the High Master, although a kind and supportive influence in Thomas's life, was, according to De Quincey, an inferior Grecian to his young charges. Bored and oppressed with life at school, Thomas desired to be allowed to use the income from a small patrimonial property he had inherited and attend Oxford at once – yet, his guardians would not allow it. In 1802 De Quincey fled from the school and walked to St John's Priory in Cheshire, where his mother was living. He was granted one guinea a week as an allowance, and he embarked on a walking tour of North Wales. Towards the close of the year, De Quincey made his way to London. His *Confessions of an English Opium-Eater* depict the troubled times that followed and the manner in which, having broken off contact with his guardians, he attempted to borrow from moneylenders against the £2,600 that he was to receive on coming of age. Delays and frustrations ensued, and De Quincey found himself on the brink of starvation and living in the rat-infested lodgings of a dubious attorney in Greek Street, Soho, with a frightened child of doubtful origin for company. He would walk the city at night, often with a girl he considered to be his guardian angel – a young prostitute named Ann. Around that time, he made a desperate trip to Eton via the Bristol mail coach to seek the aid of Howe Browne, and finding that he was away at Cambridge, he resorted to his cousin John Otway Cuffe, the future Earl of Desart. With all his attempts at obtaining his loan coming to nothing, De Quincey returned to his mother in Chester in the spring of 1803, after which he spent several months with friends in Everton.

Correspondence with Wordsworth and matriculation at Oxford

In May of that year, De Quincey wrote a letter to Wordsworth, whose poetry had first enraptured the young student several years earlier. The letter expressed his love for the *Lyrical Ballads* (1798) and "humbly" asked for the great poet's friendship. Wordsworth replied, and the two continued to correspond. Meanwhile, De Quincey entered Worcester College, Oxford, at the end of the year. Not a great deal is known of his time at Oxford, but it was in 1804, during his university days, albeit while staying in London, that De Quincey first took opium as a means of lessening the pain of a toothache. The drug then became an intermittent delight for De Quincey: his frequent visits to London often meant for him either opium and the opera or opium and late-night walks through the city.

Coleridge and Wordsworth

Twice in the ensuing years he made his way to the Lake District, at least in part to introduce himself to Wordsworth, although on both occasions he decided to postpone the visit. In 1806, on his coming of age, he received his £2,600, a considerable chunk of which was immediately used to pay debts he had accrued over the preceding years. In 1807 De Quincey, while visiting his mother in Somerset, first met Coleridge, the co-author of his beloved *Lyrical Ballads*. They swiftly became friends, and in October De Quincey accompanied Sara Coleridge and their children to their home in Keswick, in the Lakes, and on this occasion he finally met Wordsworth, as well as the poet's sister Dorothy and his wife Mary. After a brief sojourn with Wordsworth, he and the poet travelled to Keswick, where De Quincey met Robert Southey.

Dove Cottage, Death of Catharine Wordsworth and Increased Opium Consumption

De Quincey left Oxford without a degree in 1808, having failed to turn up for the second day of his examinations. In October of that year, he returned to stay with the Wordsworths, who had now left their home at Dove Cottage, Grasmere, for Allan Bank, a larger house nearby. The following October saw De Quincey take up residence in Dove Cottage, and he soon struck up friendships with the poet Charles Lloyd and the literary critic and academic John Wilson – both of whom lived nearby.

The death of William and Mary Wordsworth's daughter Catharine in 1812 at the age of three sent De Quincey, who loved her dearly and delighted in having her with him at Dove Cottage, into the depths of melancholy and grief, and he regularly passed the night on her grave. He suspected that it was his distress at Catharine's death that led him to bodily illness. This, in turn, was the catalyst for eight years' intermittent opium use, which by 1813 became far more regular.

Marriage to Margaret and Birth of William

Around that time, De Quincey began a love affair with Margaret Simpson (1796–1837), the daughter of a local farmer who lived on the banks of Rydal Water. The Wordsworths were against the match, and Dorothy reported that Margaret was "a stupid, heavy girl" and had been "reckoned a dunce at Grasmere School". De Quincey, on the other hand, spoke of Margaret's "beauty", her "good sense" and her "angelic sweetness". A child, William (named after Thomas's late brother), was born in November 1816, with seven more children to follow over the years, and Thomas and Margaret were married at Grasmere in February 1817.

Editorship of the Westmorland Gazette

In 1818, with an election approaching, Wordsworth, who was supporting the cause of the Tory Lowther family, recommended a pamphlet written anonymously by De Quincey, in which he attacked a speech made by the Whig Henry Brougham. With the editor of the Tory *Westmorland Gazette* soon proving unsatisfactory, De Quincey was offered the editorship in the summer of 1818. He remained in the post until November 1819, yet the proprietors had begun to make their unease regarding De Quincey's unreliability known before the latter eventually decided to resign his position.

Confessions of an English Opium-Eater

In December 1820, with pecuniary concerns weighing ever more heavily upon him, De Quincey accepted John Wilson's invitation to join him in writing for *Blackwood's Edinburgh Magazine* and travelled up to the Scottish capital. Soon, however, he quarrelled with the proprietor William Blackwood, and by January 1821 De Quincey had returned to the Lakes. In the summer he visited London and was taken on as a contributor by *The London Magazine*. He lodged in Covent Garden and worked on an autobiographical piece detailing aspects of his early life and the development of his opium addiction called *Confessions of an English Opium-Eater*. It was published anonymously in the September and October editions of the magazine. It garnered widespread attention and critical acclaim, and was thus published in book form in 1822. The next few years saw De Quincey write numerous pieces for *The London Magazine*, including translations of works by Immanuel Kant and the German Romantic Jean Paul.

Edinburgh In the summer of 1825, De Quincey's wife and children were evicted from their Lake District home, Fox Ghyll, and were forced to move in with Margaret's parents. In October 1826 De Quincey travelled to Edinburgh and began working once more for *Blackwood's Edinburgh Magazine* – a post he combined, from 1827, with sporadic contributions to the *Edinburgh Saturday Post*. In the winter of 1830, he brought his family, long divided from him, up to Edinburgh. Why he had not done so sooner is a mystery – Dorothy Wordsworth had earlier asked De Quincey his reasons for not bringing his family up to Edinburgh, "where lodgings are cheap", but his reply has not survived – and certainly Margaret, left alone for long periods in the Lakes with her children, was dissatisfied with the situation. Margaret had attempted suicide before she knew De Quincey, and his long absences and spiralling debts drove her into fits of gloom and melancholy. The situation appears only to have been remedied when she wrote her husband a letter informing him that if he could not find the money to pay the creditors she would kill herself.

Despite his articles now being in demand, De Quincey was continuously besieged by pecuniary problems, and he was imprisoned for debt in October 1831, only to be released again on the same day due to his fragile health. Holyrood Abbey in Edinburgh had, since the 1500s, offered sanctuary to those who were unable to pay their debts, and this right of sanctuary extended to Holyrood Park and the buildings on Abbey Strand. De Quincey was among the thousands who took advantage of the rights offered by this ancient building, and his life became a web of false names and addresses as his creditors closed in.

The Deaths of Coleridge and William De Quincey

In April 1832 his only novel, *Klosterheim, or The Masque*, was published, and February 1834 saw the publication of the first part of the 'Sketches of Life and Manners; from the Autobiography of an English Opium-Eater' in *Tait's Edinburgh Magazine*. These autobiographical writings continued to appear intermittently until 1839, and were a great success, leading to a surge in *Tait's* popularity. With the death of Coleridge in 1834, De Quincey penned four reminiscences entitled 'Samuel Taylor Coleridge', which were published in *Tait's*. The pieces, which included details of Coleridge's opium addiction and the failure of his marriage, caused the late poet's family much hurt, and it was seen as an act of betrayal, though it was, in many ways, an accurate account, as the pair had spent a significant amount of time together over the years. This period, however, brought keener woes to De Quincey than Coleridge's passing and the clamour that surrounded the reminiscences, for his eldest child William died of unknown causes in November 1834, at the age of eighteen, the same age as the late uncle after whom he was named.

The Death of Margaret De Quincey

By May 1836, De Quincey and his family were living within the Holyrood sanctuary, and on 7th August 1837 Margaret De Quincey died of typhus. Of course De Quincey felt profound and acute grief at the loss of the woman who, in his *Confessions of an English Opium-Eater*, he describes so movingly as fondly wiping "away for years the unwholesome dews" upon his forehead, refreshing "the lips when parched and baked with fever" and never withdrawing her "angelic smiles", even after all the troubles she faced through his ill health and opium addiction.

'Suspiria de profundis' and 'The English Mail Coach'

In 1840, Margaret, De Quincey's eldest daughter, took charge of his affairs, and she appears to have managed them far better than he had ever been able to. The ceaseless fear and harassment that the family had to endure during the years of debt came to an end, and a degree of stability entered De Quincey's life – broken tragically by the death of his son Horatio, a lieutenant in the army, in China. In 1845 *Blackwood's* published his 'Suspiria de profundis', the sequel to *Confessions of an English Opium-Eater*, which examines the manner in which opium acts on the memories and recollections of the dreamer. 'The English Mail Coach', widely regarded as one of his greatest works and, like the *Confessions* and 'Suspiria', an attempt to wreath and describe in language the nebulous world of dreams, also appeared in *Blackwood's* in 1849.

Last Years and Death

For many years De Quincey had vacillated between *Blackwood's* and *Tait's* in a cycle of argument and reconciliation. In 1850, however, James Hogg's *The Instructor* (*Titan* from 1856) became the principal publisher of De Quincey's works, and from 1852 onwards Hogg began to publish volume after volume of Thomas's collected works, titled *Selections Grave and Gay*. This involved revisions and additions to De Quincey's oeuvre, most notably to *Confessions of an English Opium-Eater*. The 1856 edition was almost double the length of the original and strove to explain and make explicit much of what was ambiguous or withheld in 1821, including numerous names and places. De Quincey was still occupied in revising the *Selections Grave and Gay* in the autumn of 1859 when he fell ill. He was confined to his bed and died, with his daughters Margaret and Emily at his bedside, on 8th December 1859. The exact cause of death was not recorded. Among his final words, Emily recalled that he cried out, "Sister! Sister! Sister!" Elizabeth had come to him at the end, as he stated in the 'Suspiria' that he knew she would. He was buried in the graveyard at St Cuthbert's, at the foot of Castle Rock in Edinburgh.

Thomas De Quincey's Works

Literary Reputation

Thomas De Quincey is often regarded as the last of the British Romantics, but his works, mainly pieces for magazines written in a variety of styles and on wildly varying subjects, have always been somewhat difficult to categorize. Regardless of this divergent and diffuse back catalogue, his influence over subsequent writers has been profound. One could quite plausibly assert that he created the genres of drug literature and the literature of addiction, yet his essays on murder were also extremely influential – inspiring figures as diverse as Dostoevsky, who took a copy of *Confessions* with him into exile, and Alfred Hitchcock, and with the Brontë sisters, avid readers of *Blackwood's*, growing up reading De Quincey. Indeed, his influence on Charlotte and Emily, in particular, would be clear even without Charlotte's declaration of the "pleasure and profit" they owed to him. The sisters' pseudonymous collection of poetry published in 1846 – the first of their works to go to print – was sent to Thomas De Quincey, among others, by the sisters as a complimentary gesture to one of the writers they most admired. *Wuthering Heights*, for example, owes a clear debt to De Quincey, with the dream visions, the frenzied grief, the corpse of the beloved furtively visited after death and the apparitions of the deceased loved one just a few instances in which De Quincey's influence can be felt.

Charles Baudelaire declared that his whole "emotional and aesthetic orientation" was affected by reading De Quincey's works. *Les Paradis artificiels* (1860), his book on the effects of opium and hashish, contained translations from and a commentary on *Confessions of an English Opium-Eater* and 'Suspiria de profundis'. This led to significant French interest in De Quincey – so much so that his standing in France has long been greater than it is in Britain, with his influence on the Symbolists and Surrealists contributing to this. Similarly, a collection of his works was published in the USA – where De Quincey was considered a master of his art and British magazines were held in extremely high regard – years before Hogg began the process of doing likewise in Britain, and Ralph Waldo Emerson sought out De Quincey above all others on a visit to Scotland in 1848. Nathaniel Hawthorne succinctly summarized the difference in perception between the two nations in regard to De Quincey when he lamented that "No Englishman cares a pin for De Quincey".

Along with Baudelaire, it is perhaps Edgar Allan Poe and Jorge Luis Borges who were most overtly influenced by De Quincey. Poe called the author of the *Confessions* one of the "first men in England", and Borges wondered whether he "could have existed without De Quincey".

De Quincey's oeuvre is made up predominantly of essays and German translations: yet, as there are far too many of these to treat individually, only his best-known works will be detailed here.

Confessions of an English Opium-Eater

The publication of *Confessions of an English Opium-Eater* in *The London Magazine* in 1821 was the first of De Quincey's works to garner widespread public notice. It was published in book form the following year and went through numerous editions in Britain and the USA in De Quincey's lifetime alone.

The work also had a staggering effect on the scientific community, informing medical, as well as public, thought regarding opium for decades. At the same time, the book was accused of having the pernicious effect of inspiring others to try the drug – an accusation which is parodied in Arthur Conan Doyle's Sherlock Holmes story 'The Man with the Twisted Lip' (1891), in which it is revealed that an opium addict first experimented with the drug after reading De Quincey's masterpiece. The fact that *Confessions* appeared anonymously at first also meant that there was much debate concerning the identity of the enigmatic opium-eater. Charles Lamb and Coleridge were leading suspects, yet many recognized De Quincey immediately, including the diarist Henry Crabb Robinson, who, as soon as he had read the first instalment, declared that it was "a fragment of autobiography in emulation of Coleridge's diseased egotism" and that "it must be by De Quincey". John Taylor, the proprietor of *The London Magazine*, was congratulated by the eminent publisher Charles Ollier on having the "best prose writer in England" contributing to his magazine, and the former summed up the prevailing mood when he wrote that "everybody who noticed magazines at all is interested in the fate of the opium-eater".

The work, written in what De Quincey styled "impassioned prose", is an account of the author's childhood, schooldays, the period he spent as a destitute teenager in London and his descent into the depths of opium addiction, and includes sections on the pleasures and the pains of the drug. Naturally, due to its subject matter, the work has, at times, a nebulous quality, for De Quincey is often attempting to "clothe in words the visionary scenes derived from the world of dreams".

The work had no obvious precedent in literature, and as such it is rightly considered one of the most original and influential works of the nineteenth century. However, it would be wrong to pass over the influence of Wordsworth and Coleridge in the *Confessions*. Indeed, for any writer so in the thrall of another as the young De Quincey was from the moment he first read Wordsworth, it is barely possible to set quill to paper without an echo or a certain redolence, however subtle, of the idol pouring forth. So it was with De Quincey, for the analytical focus on the growth and development of the author's mind found in the *Confessions* is highly reminiscent of *The Prelude*, whose full title is *The Prelude, or Growth of a Poet's Mind: An Autobiographical Poem*. And just as, in the latter work, Wordsworth can triumphantly state that "we have traced the stream / From darkness... followed it to light / And open day... afterwards / Lost sight of it bewildered and engulfed, / Then given it greeting as it rose once more... reflecting in its solemn breast / The works of man and face of human life", so De Quincey revisits his early life in order to answer the question: "How came any reasonable being to subject himself to such a yoke of misery, voluntarily to incur a captivity so servile and knowingly to fetter himself with such a sevenfold chain?"

Coleridge, too, shaped the young De Quincey – and if one were to talk of a writer influenced by Kant and Wordsworth, known for his opium-infused public persona, famed for his exotic, Gothic and oriental dream visions, as well as his conversational brilliance and extraordinary mind, but who failed perhaps to produce a work that lived up to the heights expected by those around him, such a description could work equally well for Coleridge or his erstwhile follower De Quincey. Coleridge did not write a work akin to the *Confessions* regarding his own opium addiction, yet the aroma of such works as 'Kubla Khan, or A Vision in a Dream: A Fragment' and 'Christabel' pervades the *Confessions*, and De Quincey undoubtedly styled himself, at least in part, on his illustrious friend.

'Suspiria de profundis'

'Suspiria de profundis', a sequel to the *Confessions of an English Opium-Eater*, was published by *Blackwood's* in 1845. It is a series of visionary explorations of themes such as childhood, sorrow and dreams, and focuses on the great grief of De Quincey's life: the death in childhood of his sister Elizabeth. The work delves into the relationship between opium and the human imagination. Dreaming, for De Quincey, is the conduit "through which man communicates with the shadowy", which "forces the infinite into the chambers of the human brain". Yet opium, through its ability to exalt "the colours of dream scenery", deepen "its shadows" and strengthen "the sense of its fearful realities", plays a crucial role in the power of dreams. As such, 'Suspiria' builds on the idea first expounded in the *Confessions*, in which De Quincey states that "there is no such thing as forgetting possible to the mind", rather a veil has been placed before these memories – a veil which opium can "rend away". Yet, opium is also, of course, an extremely destructive force, and De Quincey talks emotively in 'Suspiria' of his "third prostration before the dark idol" – in other words, having twice before successfully, for a while at least, torn himself away from his dependence on opium, before later relapsing, De Quincey, at the time of this "third prostration", became "profoundly aware" that to tear himself away once more was "impossible", as the "towering gates of ingress which hitherto had always seemed to stand open" were now barred against his retreat and "hung with funeral crape". "Upon seeing those awful gates," he continues, "I… spoke not, nor started, nor groaned. One profound sigh ascended from my heart, and I was silent for days."

At the heart of 'Suspiria', however, is the consolation that suffering and grief are necessary for the full development of the self. This is conveyed by the best-known part of the work: the remarkable prose poem 'Levana and Our Ladies of Sorrow'. Here De Quincey delves once more into his dreams and describes how the goddess Levana – the Roman goddess of childhood, associated with raising newborn infants after they had been laid on the ground after birth – visited him during his years at Oxford, along with the three Sorrows: Mater Lachrymarum, Mater Suspiriorum and Mater Tenebrarum – Our Lady of Tears, Our Lady of Sighs and Our Lady of Darkness respectively. At that time, he had known only one of the sisters, yet he was soon to be an intimate of all three, and it is through their ministrations, their banishing of hope, their scorching the "fountain of tears", that he is able to see into the heart of things: "So shall he be accomplished in the furnace, so shall he see the things that ought not to be seen, sights that are abominable and secrets that are unutterable. So shall he read elder truths, sad truths, grand truths, fearful truths. So shall he rise again before he dies. And so shall our commission be accomplished which from God we had – to plague his heart until we had unfolded the capacities of his spirit".

De Quincey halted the publication of the series in July 1845, dissatisfied with the decision made by *Blackwood's* to delay an instalment and concerned that "some unknown person at the press" was constantly doing him "the most serious injuries" in the form of unauthorized changes that made their way into the work. As with his other pieces, De Quincey made amendments and additions to 'Suspiria' prior to its publication in the *Selections Grave and Gay* that appeared through the 1850s.

'The English Mail Coach'

'The English Mail Coach' was published in *Blackwood's* in 1849 and marks perhaps the highest point of De Quincey's exploration and evocation of the opium-infused imagination. The work had been intended originally as part of 'Suspiria', yet was published separately, as two individual pieces that featured in the October and December issues of *Blackwood's*. While the pair were clearly part of a single whole, the work had no unifying title. It was in 1854, when they appeared in *Selections Grave and Gay*, that the current title was chosen.

Memories and dreams once more collide and intermingle, and mail coaches are held responsible for "developing the anarchies" of De Quincey's dreams through several principal causes: i.e., to paraphrase De Quincey, their unprecedented velocity, the grand effects for the eye between lamplight and darkness on solitary roads, the animal beauty and power of the horses and the conscious presence of a central intellect that overcomes all obstacles into one steady cooperation to a national result and acts as the national organ for spreading the news of mighty events such as the victory at Waterloo.

De Quincey proceeds to expound upon and illustrate these points before, in 'The Vision of Sudden Death', the second part of the work, he descends once more into the slough of terror and nightmares as he recalls how he had sat, warm with opium, next to the driver of the mail coach. The latter appeared as a monstrous one-eyed creature who soon fell into a deep sleep, as did the guard – and De Quincey, despite the peril of his situation, settled into a profound repose. On hearing the distant murmur of an approaching vehicle, however, De Quincey calls out to rouse the attention of an oncoming pair of lovers, and the man, seizing the reins, narrowly manages to avoid a fatal head-on collision. Yet the spectacle of the woman during those climactic moments continues to haunt De Quincey's dreams, with her arms thrown up "wildly to heaven", while "Death, the crowned phantom", amidst the "flashing of cataracts", leapt upon her with roaring "tiger" voice.

In *Confessions of an English Opium-Eater*, 'Suspiria de profundis' and 'The English Mail Coach', De Quincey created a pioneering form of autobiography that sought to understand the makings of the self, and in particular the genesis of the dreams and addictions that haunted him, through experiences and memories that were often veiled but for the agency of "just, subtle and mighty opium". In doing so, De Quincey's unique subject matter, his extraordinary mind and his vibrant prose, which Virginia Woolf described as travelling "down to us from great heights, reverberating with strange thunders", saw him ascend above what he lambasted as the "utter sterility" of the literature that had hitherto dealt with dreams and visions.

Select Bibliography

Biographies:

Lindop, Grevel, *The Opium-Eater: A Life of Thomas De Quincey* (London: Dent, 1981)

Morrison, Robert, *The English Opium-Eater: A Biography of Thomas De Quincey* (London, Weidenfeld and Nicolson, 2009)

Wilson, Frances, *Guilty Thing: A Life of Thomas De Quincey* (London: Bloomsbury, 2016)

Additional Recommended Background Material:

Baxter, Edmund, *De Quincey's Art of Autobiography* (Edinburgh: Edinburgh University Press, 1990).

Bridgwater, Patrick, *De Quincey's Gothic Masquerade* (New York: Rodopi, 2004)

Clej, Alina, *A Genealogy of the Modern Self: Thomas De Quincey and the Intoxication of Writing* (Stanford, CA: Stanford University Press, 1995)

McDonagh, Josephine, *De Quincey's Disciplines* (Oxford: Clarendon Press, 1994)

Morrison, Robert and Roberts, Daniel Sanjiv, eds., *Thomas De Quincey: New Theoretical and Critical Directions* (New York: Routledge, 2008)